The Cooking Ladies'
Recipes from the Road

The Cooking Ladies'
Recipes from the Road

Stovetop Creations and Travel Adventures

Phyllis Hinz and Lamont Mackay

TEN SPEED PRESS
Berkeley | Toronto

Ten Speed Press
P.O. Box 7123
Berkeley, California 94707
www.tenspeed.com

Distributed in Australia by Simon & Schuster Australia, in Canada by Ten Speed Press Canada, in New Zealand by Southern Publishers Group, in South Africa by Real Books, and in the United Kingdom and Europe by Airlift Book Company.

Photography by Phyllis Hinz and Lamont Mackay
Cover design by Chloe Rawlins
Interior design by Artplus

First published by RFTR Pulishing (Canada) in 2003.

Library of Congress Cataloging-in-Publication Data

Hinz, Phyllis, 1946–
    The cooking ladies' recipes from the road : stovetop creations and travel adventures / Phyllis Hinz, Lamont Mackay.
        p. cm.
    Includes index.
    ISBN-10: 1-58008-672-1 (pbk.)
    ISBN-13: 978-1-58008-672-1 (pbk.)
    1. Cookery. I. Mackay, Lamont, 1945– II. Title.

TX714.H557 2005
641.5—dc22

2004062096

First printing, 2005
Printed in China

1 2 3 4 5 6 7 8 9 10 — 09 08 07 06 05

For Susan Emmott

Table of Contents

Sandwiches

Eggs

Pasta

Chicken

Beef

Pork

Seafood

Vegetables

Desserts

Drinks

Introduction

We met in 1975 during a writing class at the University of British Columbia. Phyllis was on her way to a Fine Arts degree in Creative Writing. Lamont, a high school English teacher, was taking a course to upgrade her skills. Our first food related partnership was a collaboration to make deviled eggs for a class picnic.

In 1977, we set out on an adventure that would change our lives forever. Our plan was to tour Europe in a Volkswagen van. We depleted our travel funds by taking five weeks to drive from British Columbia to Ontario via California and Florida. Needing jobs, we took on the task of running the kitchen of a small hotel in Dublin, Ontario. One year later, with enough cash to continue our journey, we set out on a nine-month adventure to sample the cuisines of Europe.

In 1979, we formed a business partnership and began a career as restaurateurs. For the next sixteen years, we successfully owned and operated restaurants and a catering company. Our various endeavors included a family-style restaurant specializing in German food; an upscale intimate dining establishment; a fish-and-chip restaurant; a soup, salad, and sandwich operation; and an off-premises catering company. Retirement from the daily demands of restaurant ownership lead to spin-off careers as food columnists and restaurant consultants.

To satisfy our appetite for adventure we sold our houses and most of our possessions and on August 20, 1998, we moved into a motorhome and took our computers on the road.

This is not just another cookbook. This cookbook will bring the tastes of travel into your kitchen as you sample recipes from some of the interesting places we have visited. Read the accompanying stories and do some armchair traveling at the same time.

Our Date at the China Ranch

The desire to sample a date milkshake lured us to the China Ranch Date Farm near Tecopa and Death Valley, California. We drove along a narrow, winding roadway through a canyon with high, over-hanging gravel cliffs that could best be described as intimidating. A great spot for an ambush in a western movie. We felt vulnerable in our little car. The motorhome was parked safely at a friend's house. It would have had a difficult time with the curves and slopes.

The China Ranch Date Farm has a lawless and interesting history. During the 1880s, numerous Chinese laborers worked in the borax industry in the area. One particular Chinese man came to the canyon and developed a water source. He planted fruit and vegetables and raised meat for the local mining camps. His settlement became known as the Chinaman's Ranch.

Sometime in 1900, a man named Morrison ran the Chinese farmer off at gunpoint and claimed the ranch for his own. The Chinese farmer was never heard of again. The land changed hands several times, but the name China Ranch remained. The daughter of a Death Valley pioneer planted the original date grove, from seed, in the early 1920s.

Today, the ranch is a working family farm in a truly unusual setting. The present owners have built a 4,500-square-foot (1,372-square-meter) adobe house in their lush oasis in the Mojave Desert. They used over eighteen thousand hand-made bricks manufactured from materials found on the ranch.

This date yogurt sauce is rich and delicious. In fact, it tastes similar to the date shake that we enjoyed at the date farm.

Date Yogurt Condiment

(Makes approximately 2 cups)

1 cup	*240 ml*	*pitted dates*
10 tablespoons	*150 ml*	*water*
1 cup	*240 ml*	*low-fat plain yogurt*
¼ teaspoon	*1.25 ml*	*salt*

Rinse the dates in a strainer. Place them in a saucepan with the water over medium-high heat. When the water boils, turn the heat to medium-low. Cook the dates for 5 minutes. While they cook, stir them with a fork, mashing them as they soften.

When the dates are soft and mushy, transfer them to a bowl and set it into the refrigerator to cool.

Add the yogurt to the chilled dates. Add the salt. Mix well and refrigerate.

This condiment is tasty with either hot or cold pork.

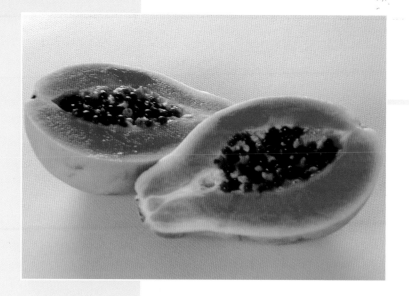

Miami Produces Football-Sized Papayas

Super Bowl wasn't the only excitement in Miami in 1999. We window-shopped in Coconut Grove, pondered the pedestrian parade in front of the art deco hotels of South Beach, and ate Cuban food in Little Havana. We drove along residential streets where wrought-iron bars fortify doors and windows and air conditioners; where lush, tropical trees and jungle vines hang down into laneways and backyards.

The outlying districts of the city are rich with vegetable and fruit farms. Oranges, tomatoes, key limes, grapefruit, mangoes, and papayas fill monstrous bins at local farmers' markets. At the Fruit and Spice Park, south of Miami, we wandered the lush thirty-two-acre park where we learned that when the bark of the cinnamon tree is cut and dried it naturally forms the curled up sticks that we buy in grocery stores.

The Fruit and Spice Park showcases over five hundred varieties of exotic fruits, herbs, spices, and nuts. Some of the species were familiar and some very foreign and exotic. We sampled star fruit, grapefruit, custard apples, litchi, bananas, and papayas right from the trees.

The south Florida papaya trees produce football-size fruit. The final thrill of our visit to Miami was to tackle such a papaya and touch down with a winning recipe. This is an excellent marinade for steak, chicken, or pork chops. Boiling blends the ingredients of this marinade into a delicious chutney.

Papaya Marinade and Chutney

(Serves 2 to 4)

1 cup	240 ml	fresh ripe papaya
2 tablespoons	30 ml	fresh lime juice
2 tablespoons	30 ml	soy sauce
1 tablespoon	15 ml	honey
1 teaspoon	5 ml	Louisiana hot sauce
1 teaspoon	5 ml	coarse black pepper
2 tablespoons	30 ml	extra virgin olive oil
2 tablespoons	30 ml	balsamic vinegar

Wash the outer skin of the papaya and cut it in half, lengthwise. Remove the seeds, peel the papaya, and cut the fruit into cubes. Place the cubes in a bowl and mash with a fork.

Add the lime juice, soy sauce, honey, hot sauce, black pepper, olive oil, and balsamic vinegar to the mashed papaya and mix well.

Place steaks, pork chops, or chicken breasts in an airtight container; pour the marinade over the meat and seal. Set in the refrigerator for 8 to 24 hours. Turn the meat over twice through the marinating time. If the marinade gels after it has chilled, spread it over the top and sides of the meat with a knife.

Remove the meat from the marinade. The marinade can be served with the meat as a chutney but it must be well cooked. Immediately place the marinade in a saucepan and bring it to a boil. Stir it well and boil for 5 minutes. Cooking destroys bacteria from the raw meat.

Cook the meat and serve with the hot papaya chutney.

This Peach Barbecue Sauce Is Divine

We got our kicks on Route 66 and, at the same time, took a cruise down memory lane. Kingman, Arizona, lies in the heart of the longest remaining stretch of historic Route 66. The town is a journey back in time to art deco signs, roadside cafes, and mom-and-pop motels.

Andy Devine, an actor known for his high, squeaky voice and large girth, grew up in Kingman. The Hotel Beale, on Route 66, was owned and operated by his parents. Andy moved to Hollywood where he became known as the loveable sidekick to western heroes like Roy Rogers. He is probably best remembered from television as Jingles on *The Wild Bill Hickok Show*.

After a hard day's drive on the RV trail, we slow-cooked a side of pork ribs and smothered them in this peach barbecue sauce. Andy would have enjoyed our meal after a day of ribbing in the saddle.

Peach Barbecue Sauce

(Makes approximately 2 cups)

3½ cups	840 ml	canned, sliced peaches with liquid (not clingstone)
1 cup	240 ml	orange juice
1 cup	240 ml	corn syrup or honey
2 teaspoons	10 ml	crushed red pepper flakes
2 tablespoons	30 ml	Worcestershire sauce
3 tablespoons	45 ml	ketchup
1 teaspoon	5 ml	ground white pepper
2 tablespoons	30 ml	Dijon mustard
2 tablespoons	30 ml	minced instant onion flakes
2 teaspoons	10 ml	minced fresh ginger
4	4	large cloves garlic, minced
2 tablespoons	30 ml	soy sauce
3 tablespoons	45 ml	cider vinegar

Partially break up the peaches with a fork. Do not discard the liquid.

Combine the peaches, peach liquid, orange juice, corn syrup, red pepper flakes, Worcestershire sauce, ketchup, white pepper, mustard, onion flakes, ginger, garlic, soy sauce, and cider vinegar in a heavy saucepan.

Slow boil the mixture, uncovered, over medium-low heat for 30 minutes. Stir often.

The sauce will reduce to about half.

Press the cooked sauce through a sieve.

Leftover barbecue sauce can be refrigerated for up to 1 week. It is good on chicken or ribs.

Signs of Spring Turn into a Simple Rhubarb Recipe

The second sign of spring in the Texas Rio Grande Valley is the mass exodus of motorhomes. License plates from places like Minnesota, Michigan, Manitoba, Iowa, Wisconsin, South Dakota, and Saskatchewan wind their way through the brush country of the Deep South in the direction of their homes up north.

The first sign of spring is the stockpiling of fresh produce to take on the trip. At Rio Grande Valley markets, bright orange mesh bags of Rio Red grapefruit are loaded into the trunks of cars, backs of pick-up trucks, and basements of motorhomes. Texas 1015 onions are wheeled by the cartload across dusty parking lots to be loaded into backseats. The vendors of Texas Mars oranges offer free samples. At a nod from a customer, money is exchanged and a bag is hoisted onto a young shoulder ready to follow the Winter Texan to his or her vehicle. The trunk of our towed car will hold three 25-pound bags of grapefruit, one 10-pound bag of oranges, and one 50-pound bag of Texas sweet onions, if we remove the golf clubs.

Each year, as the chilly northern weather gives way to warmer temperatures and sunny skies, tens of thousands of winter residents depart the Valley. They leave behind their winter walks on the beach, shopping trips to Mexico, golf, bingo, and dancing. They reach their northern homes when the last winter storm is hopefully just a memory and the first bright pink shoots of rhubarb are pushing through the recently sun-warmed soil.

Rhubarb Condiment

(Serves 4)

2 cups	480 ml	fresh or frozen rhubarb
3 tablespoons	45 ml	cider vinegar
¼ cup	60 ml	brown sugar
¼ cup	60 ml	white sugar
½ teaspoon	2.5 ml	ground cinnamon
1 cup	240 ml	unsweetened applesauce

Wash the rhubarb and trim away any leaves and tough ends. Cut the shoots into ¼- to ½-inch pieces.

Combine the cider vinegar, brown sugar, white sugar, and cinnamon in a saucepan. Place the saucepan over medium heat and stir until the mixture is smooth.

Add the rhubarb and stir until it is broken up. Stir in the applesauce.

Serve with chicken, pork, or beef.

The Red Hat Society

We were sitting in a restaurant when twelve women walked in wearing red hats and purple dresses. They caused a scene and they seemed to love it. The women were members of the Red Hat Society.

The Red Hat Society is fondly described as a "disorganization" by its creator, Sue Ellen Cooper of California. She and a few friends took inspiration from a poem entitled "Warning" by Jenny Joseph. The poem begins "When I am an old woman I shall wear purple, with a red hat that doesn't go and doesn't suit me."

The philosophy of the Red Hat Society is a belief that silliness is the comic relief of life, and that women who share a bond of affection forged by common life experiences and a genuine enthusiasm for life should join red-gloved hands and "go for the gusto."

The rules of the club sound simple. If a woman is fifty or older, she wears a purple outfit and a red hat. If she is under fifty, she wears a pink hat with an outfit as close to lavender as she can find. The only other rule is that there are no rules, except to get together and have a good time.

Most of the almost six thousand chapters of the Red Hat Society are in Canada and the United States. Others are in the United Kingdom, Australia, New Zealand, and Mexico. Four members of "The Young and the Wreckless" chapter in Florida sport a permanent tattoo of the club's logo on upper thighs, a lower leg, and a chest. One of the women, a seventy-one-year-old, reported that her husband loves it.

Like the Red Hatters, we went for the gusto when we created this recipe. It's a great accessory for lamb.

Sun-Dried Tomato Condiment

(Serves 4)

12	12	sun-dried tomatoes
		warm water
2 tablespoons	30 ml	diced onion
4	4	cloves garlic
1 tablespoon	15 ml	chopped lemon, with peel
1 tablespoon	15 ml	canola oil
1	1	beef bouillon cube
¼ teaspoon	1.25 ml	black pepper

Place the sun-dried tomatoes in a bowl with enough warm water to cover. Soak for 15 minutes.

Save the tomato water. Cut the softened tomatoes into bite-sized pieces.

Finely dice the onion.

Peel and thinly slice the garlic.

Remove any seeds from the lemon and finely chop both the flesh and the peel.

Heat the oil in a frying pan over medium heat and add the sun-dried tomato, onion, garlic, and lemon. Stir to combine the ingredients.

When the onion is translucent, add 1 cup (240 ml) of the reserved tomato water and the bouillon cube. Top up with tap water if there is not enough tomato water. Stir to dissolve the bouillon cube. Add the pepper.

Turn the heat to a slow boil for 5 to 8 minutes to blend the flavors and to reduce the liquid.

Remove the sauce from the heat and serve hot over cooked lamb chops.

This condiment can also be refrigerated and served on crackers.

A Recipe from the Rain forest

"The Puerto Rican boa can reach a length of seven and a half feet, but I make trips out here every day and I've never seen one," said Gus, our tour guide. We kept a watch for logs that moved just in case this was the day one decided to appear. Gus assured us that there weren't any poisonous snakes as he pointed to the wild orchids, giant ferns, and rare trees of the El Yunque Rain Forest.

El Yunque, twenty-eight thousand acres of highly dense vegetation, receives two hundred inches of rain per year. "Rain is predictable up here. It can be sunny and beautiful and then suddenly dark rain clouds appear," Gus said as we hiked behind him.

The Puerto Rican parrot, a bright green bird with blue primary wing feathers, is on the endangered species list. There are approximately eighty-five birds in existence. Tiny coquis, tree frogs, are indigenous to the forest. Sierra Palm trees add softness as they stand tall with fronds that look like gigantic ferns.

As an official tour guide, Gus knows the forest intimately. A friend of his, an iguana, posed for our cameras. Gus knew just where to stand in order to see a new blossom on a bird of paradise.

Every year, approximately one million people make the one-hour drive from San Juan to the rain forest. Banana palms lean over the narrow road that winds up the mountain.

Banana Dippers

(Makes 30 to 35 dippers)

½ teaspoon	2.5 ml	salt
8 tablespoons	120 ml	all-purpose flour
2	2	bananas
1 tablespoon	15 ml	olive oil
		sour cream

Combine the salt and flour in a small bowl. Be sure they are thoroughly mixed.

Peel and mash the bananas. Whip the mashed bananas with a fork until smooth.

Add the flour to the bananas and mix well again.

Spread the oil evenly over the bottom of a large frying pan and heat to medium-high.

Using a teaspoon, drop the banana mixture into the frying pan. Fill the teaspoon about one-third full lengthwise; the mixture should cook in an oval shape.

Brown the banana dippers to a golden brown on both sides, just like pancakes. When the dippers are ready to flip to the second side, reduce the heat to medium.

Place the sour cream in a small bowl. Serve the banana dippers hot or cold with the sour cream as a dip.

Skagway and the Highway to It Are Spectacular

The South Klondike Highway passes waterfalls, lakes, ancient twisted trees that cling to rocks polished smooth by prehistoric glaciers, and the world's smallest desert. The highway ends at Skagway, Alaska, the gateway to the Klondike Gold Rush of 1898.

The population of Skagway has dwindled from the tens of thousands of gold-frenzied fortune-seeking prospectors to its present eight hundred year-round residents. False-fronted, Gold Rush–era buildings line the boardwalks of the historic business district where present-day shops have a reputation for the best shopping in Alaska. Customers arrive by cruise ship, train, car, and RV.

In 1898, prospectors were lured by saloons, painted ladies, and quick-fingered gamblers. We ate lunch at the Red Onion Saloon, once an exclusive brothel. The fun and excitement of the earlier days is still alive in the bustle and décor of the main floor saloon, now the restaurant. A narrow staircase climbs to ten small rooms where ladies with names like Birdie Ash, Popcorn Lil, and Babe Davenport quenched more than the prospector's thirst.

This is our version of the curried halibut salad on the Red Onion Saloon's menu.

Curried Halibut

(Serves 4 to 6)

3 cups	720 ml	water
¾ cup	180 ml	onion, cut in large pieces
¾ cup	180 ml	carrot, cut in large pieces
½	½	lemon, cut in half
14 ounces	397 g	halibut fillet
1 teaspoon	5 ml	medium curry powder
½ teaspoon	2.5 ml	salt
6 tablespoons	90 ml	mayonnaise
¼ cup	60 ml	craisins (sweetened, dried cranberries)
3 tablespoons	45 ml	chopped pecans
		pita bread

Bring the water to a boil in a saucepan. Add the onion, carrot, and lemon. Boil for 20 minutes.

Decrease the heat to a slow boil with the water gently breaking the surface. Add the halibut fillet. Be sure the fillet is completely covered with water. Poach the halibut for 5 to 10 minutes, until the flesh is white and firm.

Place the poached fillet on a plate, cover, and refrigerate to cool. Discard the onion, carrot, lemon, and liquid.

When cooled, remove and discard the skin from the fillet. Place the fish in a bowl and break it into fine pieces with a fork.

Add the curry powder and salt. Stir in the mayonnaise, 1 tablespoon at a time. Stop adding the mayonnaise when the texture is spreadable. Mix well. Add the craisins and chopped pecans and combine thoroughly.

Warm the pita bread by placing it in a frying pan over medium heat. Remove the pita bread from the frying pan to a cutting board and cut into small triangles. Place the curried halibut in a small dish on a plate and circle it with the pita bread triangles.

New Flavors for Traditional Deviled Eggs

Symbols that are scratched or carved into the veneer of a rock, probably by the use of another rock, are called petroglyphs.

We found petroglyphs along a dry riverbed while hiking in the Arizona desert. We stopped to rest beside a large mound of rock. Above our heads, clusters of lines and circles were scattered over the rock's surface. Some of the symbols looked like the jagged designs that we paint on the shells of hard-boiled Easter eggs.

In Arizona, the petroglyphs are believed to be thousands of years old. They can be found on rock faces in areas where early man paused long enough to record events, leave directions, create a supernatural message, or maybe even write recipes.

In the quiet of the desert we appreciated the shade that the rock provided from the sun and the sips of cold water from our water bottles. It was humbling to look up at the petroglyphs and realize that thousands of years earlier a group of people had stopped at the same spot, perhaps for the same reasons.

We offer these two recipes to transport your tastebuds to a new era of deviled egg flavor. You can multiply the quantities in the recipes to suit your needs.

Deviled Eggs

Tuna Deviled Eggs

(Serves 4)

2	2	eggs
1 tablespoon	15 ml	tuna, drained and flaked
1 tablespoon	15 ml	mayonnaise
1 teaspoon	5 ml	finely chopped bread-and-butter pickles
½ teaspoon	2.5 ml	fresh lemon juice

Waldorf Deviled Eggs

(Serves 4)

2	2	eggs
1 tablespoon	15 ml	mayonnaise
4 teaspoons	20 ml	finely chopped apple
1½ teaspoons	7.5 ml	finely chopped peanuts or walnuts
½ teaspoon	2.5 ml	fresh lemon juice

Cover the eggs with cold water in a saucepan over high heat. Bring the water to a boil and remove the saucepan from the heat. Tightly cover the saucepan and let it stand for 20 minutes. Drain the hot water off the eggs and cover the eggs with cold water to stop the cooking.

Peel the hardboiled eggs and slice them in half, lengthwise. Place the yolks in a bowl and rinse the whites under clear water. Turn the whites upside down on a paper towel to dry.

Mash the yolks with a fork. Add the ingredients for either the tuna or Waldorf deviled eggs and mix thoroughly.

Fill the cavities in the egg whites with the flavored yolk mixture.

Garage Sales for Diesel Fuel

When we made the decision to travel in a motorhome, we sold our houses and held garage sales to downsize our stuff. We were so excited about the roads we would travel, the people we would meet, and the sights we would see, it wasn't difficult to part with our possessions. Especially the ones tucked away in cupboards and under beds, unnoticed for years. Each garage sale served as an appetizer for the next. By the end of the ninth garage sale we were pros.

Dealers always arrived with the first glimpse of the sun. They inspected furniture, jewelry, and quilts before we had finished our first cup of coffee. By midmorning the weekend garage sale enthusiasts were rooting through our twenty-five-cent, fifty-cent, and one-dollar boxes. They checked out clothing, china, towels, and glassware and offered half of the prices we were asking. We plugged in vacuums, dehumidifiers, and calculators in order to demonstrate their condition. We loaded ladders, boards, and bricks into the trunks of cars. Neighbors arrived to encourage us to travel while we were young. When our inventory in the driveway began to dwindle, we ran into the house for more. We dragged out things that we had intended to keep and gave them a price. We were on a roll.

We added the words "Everything must go" to the signs at the street corners. We became so merciless in our quest to rid ourselves of stuff that, when we threw a farewell party for ourselves and invited all our closest friends and relatives, we held a silent raffle for the few treasures that had survived the garage sales. The proceeds went toward diesel fuel for the motorhome.

This ginger eggplant appetizer recipe is a treasure worth keeping.

Ginger Eggplant Appetizer

(Serves 6 to 8)

3 tablespoons	45 ml	finely chopped fresh ginger
2 tablespoons	30 ml	finely chopped onion
2 tablespoons	30 ml	finely chopped garlic
5 tablespoons	75 ml	soy sauce
5 tablespoons	75 ml	white sugar
1 teaspoon	5 ml	hoisin sauce
6 tablespoons	90 ml	rice vinegar
1	1	medium-large eggplant (about 10 inches long)
		nonstick olive oil cooking spray
		salt and pepper

In a medium saucepan, mix the chopped ginger, chopped onion, chopped garlic, soy sauce, sugar, hoisin sauce, and vinegar. Stir well and bring to a boil until the sugar dissolves.

Simmer and stir until thick and syrupy. Remove from the heat and set aside.

Peel the eggplant. Cut lengthwise into ⅛-inch thick slices. Brush both sides of each slice with olive oil.

Heat a frying pan over medium-high heat. Cook the eggplant on both sides until dark brown. Transfer the eggplant to paper towels to absorb any excess oil. Discard the paper towels.

Sprinkle the eggplant with salt and pepper. Cut the eggplant into ¾- to 1-inch pieces. Add the eggplant to the ginger sauce.

Stir well. Spoon the eggplant mixture into a serving bowl and refrigerate.

Serve cold with crackers.

Pickles Prompts Pickleball Game

Joel Pritchard invented the game of pickleball in 1965 when he was the Lieutenant Governor of the state of Washington. He created the game in an attempt to entertain his children on a summer day. Today, there are more than one hundred thousand pickleball enthusiasts worldwide.

The repeated pop of the perforated plastic pickleball as it hits the oversized ping-pong paddles is an early morning indicator of the popularity of the game. Sports stores can't keep up with the demand for the special twenty-six-holed balls and paddles. The game has been described as something in between badminton and tennis with a tennis-style net. It can be played on any hard surface.

Pickleball is named after the Pritchard's dog, Pickles, who according to family stories, often ran away with the ball. The name of the game may sound wimpy, but it provides a serious low-impact workout. Easy to learn, it's a sport that all ages play. The U.S.A. Pickleball Association claims the game builds self-esteem in young people, provides competitive competition for active athletes, and is like a fountain of youth for older players. If the cheering, applause, and carrying-on in the pickleball courts are any indication, the claim is true.

We received similar cheering and carrying on when we created these marinated mushrooms.

Marinated Mushrooms Italia

(Serves 4)

2 cups	480 ml	small white mushrooms
1 tablespoon	15 ml	olive oil
½	½	small onion, finely chopped
1	1	large clove garlic, finely chopped
¼ cup	60 ml	diced tomatoes with juice
¼ cup	60 ml	dry red wine
1 teaspoon	5 ml	dried oregano leaves
¼ teaspoon	1.25 ml	salt
¼ teaspoon	1.25 ml	pepper

Clean the mushrooms thoroughly with a mushroom brush or paper towel. Trim off any long stems.

Heat the olive oil in a medium saucepan. Add the onion and garlic. Cook and stir over medium heat until the onion is translucent.

Stir in the diced tomatoes, wine, oregano, salt, and pepper. Bring the mixture to a boil.

Add the mushrooms and turn down the heat to a slow boil. Cook for 5 minutes.

Refrigerate. Allow the mushrooms to marinate at least 1 hour before serving.

The Charm of St. Jacobs

St. Jacobs, Ontario, is a place where the past and present mingle, where motorhomes and cars share the roads and parking lots with horse-drawn vehicles.

The village has 1,400 inhabitants, but 1.5 million people visit annually, lured by glassblowers, potters, weavers, jewelers, broom makers, blacksmiths, painters, and quilters. Visitors stroll along the streets and explore the shops for furniture, clothing, baked goods, crafts, angels, and antiques. They savor the famous Waterloo County cuisine and embrace the rural charm of the Old Order Mennonites. In St. Jacobs, modern commercialism coexists with the simplicity of the Old World Mennonite lifestyle.

Mennonite and German influences are evident on menus in the village and in the surrounding communities. Fresh baking, farmer's sausage, spare ribs, sauerkraut, mashed potatoes, schnitzel, hearty soups, and pigtails are always available.

"What are pigtails?" This is the most frequently asked question when we introduce out-of-town friends to St. Jacobs. Even when we explain that pigtails really are pigs' tails that are slow-cooked in brown sugar, they seldom believe us. We inevitably have to take our guests on a countryside pub tour to sample the tasty morsels.

Our pickled pigtails are also tasty. They make an interesting addition to a picnic basket.

Pickled Pigtails

(Serves 6)

6	6	pigtails, about 8 inches long
2 cups	480 ml	white vinegar
2 cups	480 ml	water
1 teaspoon	5 ml	salt
1 teaspoon	5 ml	black pepper
1 teaspoon	5 ml	garlic powder
2	2	bay leaves

Wash the pigtails and cut away any large pieces of visible fat. Do not remove skin from the tail ends.

In a large pot, cover the tails completely with water. Cover the pot and boil the tails over medium to medium-high heat for 2½ hours.

While the tails are cooking, combine the vinegar, water, salt, pepper, garlic powder, and bay leaves in a small saucepan. Bring the mixture to a boil, then remove it from the heat and allow it to cool.

Drain the pigtails and place them side-by-side in a large, flat glass or plastic container. Let the pigtails cool at room temperature for about 15 minutes.

Pour the vinegar mixture over the pigtails. Cover and refrigerate for 24 to 48 hours, turning the pigtails occasionally.

Serve the pickled pigtails whole, with crackers and plenty of finger wipes.

Something Special about Strawberries

Our only bad experience with strawberries took place on an airplane bound for Mexico. The plane dropped suddenly in an air pocket and then tipped to one side—ours. Dinner had just been served. We were seated on the receiving end of all the strawberry shortcake from the six to eight seats above us. When the plane righted itself, strawberry shortcake clung to the window and dripped down the wall onto our purses and shoes. The incident didn't squash our love of strawberries, but it made us a little leery about the return flight home.

We think one of the best strawberry experiences happens every year in Plant City, Florida. According to the festival organizers at the Strawberry Festival in Plant City, the average North American eats a little more than three pounds of strawberries in a year. A cup of these berries provides a person's entire daily requirement of vitamin C. A strawberry is the only fruit with seeds on the outside, approximately two hundred of them. In the early days, Iroquois Indians used the berries to season meat and make soup. They even made tea from the leaves.

Strawberries also make a pretty garnish for our scallop appetizer.

Cream-of-the-Crop Scallops

(Serves 3)

1 tablespoon	15 ml	butter or margarine
9	9	large sea scallops
1 tablespoon	15 ml	spreadable herb-and-garlic cream cheese
½ tablespoon	7.5 ml	Dijon mustard
¼ cup	60 ml	whipping cream
½ tablespoon	7.5 ml	white wine
2 tablespoons	30 ml	crumbled blue cheese
3	3	large strawberries

Melt half of the butter in a medium frying pan. Cook and turn the scallops for 4 minutes, or until they are opaque and still soft and tender. Transfer the scallops to a plate and set aside until the sauce is prepared.

In a medium frying pan, melt the remaining half of the butter. As the butter melts add the spreadable cream cheese and mustard. Whisk until the combination is smooth.

Add the whipping cream, stir, and bring to a boil.

Stir in the wine. Add the cooked scallops. Stir to warm the scallops and then immediately remove the pan from the heat. The scallops will become rubbery if over cooked.

Place the scallops on 3 scallop-shaped dishes or on small plates with leaf lettuce. Sprinkle the crumbled blue cheese around the scallops. Pour the cream sauce over the scallops. Garnish with a strawberry.

The Lucky Turtles of South Padre Island

Ila Loetscher, the Turtle Lady of South Padre Island, Texas, began defending endangered sea turtles in the mid 1960s when turtle cowboy boots, turtle soup, and other turtle products were popular. She rescued sick and injured sea turtles from sharks, boat propellers, and abusive human poachers, taking the sea creatures to her home just a block away from the Gulf of Mexico.

Rather than a garden in her backyard, Ila had several large tanks of seawater with a row of bleachers for public viewing. She encouraged people to visit her turtles and learn about their history and the need for their preservation.

The Kemp's Ridley sea turtle is the most endangered species in the South Padre Island area. In 1947, there were more than fifty thousand females. These numbers were reduced to four hundred by 1975. Out of one hundred eggs per female, buried in the sand on the beach, only one may survive to return to the sea.

Trash and litter pose a serious threat to the air-breathing creatures. To the turtle, plastic bags look like jellyfish, one of their favorite snacks. With a brain the size of a human's little finger, a two-thousand-pound turtle needs human protectors like Ila.

We met the ninety-year-old woman several years ago. Her face was tanned and weathered to the texture of turtle skin. She held a seventy-five-pound, green sea turtle in her arms. Ila died recently, but her work continues. Injured and lost turtles are still brought regularly to her doorstep where they are cared for by Sea Turtle, Inc., an organization Ila founded in 1977.

These fried shrimp balls are fun appetizers. We're certain even the turtles would like them.

Fried Shrimp Balls with Orange Dip

(Makes approximately 25)

1 cup	240 ml	sour cream
¼ cup	60 ml	finely chopped grated orange peel
¼ teaspoon	1.25 ml	salt
1 teaspoon	5 ml	white sugar or sugar substitute
30	30	medium to large shrimp, shelled, deveined, and cooked
1	1	egg
¼ cup	60 ml	finely chopped onion
1 tablespoon	15 ml	cornstarch
½ teaspoon	2.5 ml	ground ginger
½ cup	120 ml	canola oil

Combine the sour cream, orange peel, salt, and sugar. Mix well.

Refrigerate the orange dip for at least 1 hour to blend the flavors.

Dry the shrimp on paper towels. Chop the shrimp into small pieces.

Lightly beat the egg.

Combine the chopped shrimp, chopped onion, cornstarch, and ground ginger. Add the beaten egg and mix well.

Shape the mixture into tiny balls approximately 1 inch in diameter. If the mixture is too moist to hold its shape, add a little more cornstarch.

In a wok or heavy saucepan, heat the oil over medium heat. Fry 6 to 8 shrimp balls at a time in the hot oil.

Gently turn the shrimp balls until they are golden brown on all sides. Be careful of splattering oil.

Place the browned shrimp balls on paper towels to drain.

Serve warm or cold with the orange dip.

The Dempster Challenge

The Dempster Highway runs 756 kilometers (470 miles) north from the Klondike Highway to Inuvik in the Northwest Territories. It has a reputation for chewing tires to pieces. Rumors say the highway offers a guaranteed windshield replacement. For this reason we parked our forty-foot motorhome in Whitehorse, in the Yukon, and rented a twenty-one-foot Class C motorhome from Fraserway RV Rentals.

There was heavy rain for twelve days prior to our trip up the Dempster Highway. As a result, the gravel road consisted of more potholes than road. In some places the potholes ranged from the width of a kitchen sink to a bathtub. There were two ferry crossings where the deep, slushy gravel created a challenge similar to driving through a snow bank.

Traffic on the Dempster was so sparse that we could stop in the middle of the highway and talk for half an hour to an oncoming traveler who had already made the trek to the end of the road. We drove so slowly that we were passed by a Spanish tourist on a bicycle. When we arrived in Inuvik, the roads were paved and our rattling and vibrating stopped. The only sound was the mud flying from our wheelwells.

Fraserway RV Rentals recommends that adventurers rent a truck and camper for the Dempster Highway, but the twenty-one-foot Class C motorhome worked perfectly for us. We made the round trip without a flat tire or a broken windshield. The Dempster was a challenge, but we conquered it and we'll never be the same. Without the Dempster we wouldn't have crossed the Arctic Circle, visited Inuvik, or flown to Tuktoyaktuk on the Arctic Ocean. We can't wait to do the entire trip again.

The following recipe is great for celebrations of any kind. The dips offer alternatives to the standard cocktail sauce.

Tipsy Shrimp Cocktail

(Serves 6)

30	30	uncooked medium to large shrimp
¼ cup	60 ml	fresh lemon juice
¼ cup	60 ml	dry vermouth

Peel and devein the shrimp. Leave the tails attached.

In a deep frying pan, mix the lemon juice with the vermouth. Bring the liquid to a boil over high heat. Drop the shrimp into the boiling liquid.

Cook the shrimp for about 1 minute, turning them over quickly to cook on both sides. Do not overcook the shrimp.

Remove the cooked shrimp from the pan and discard the cooking liquid.

Immediately toss the shrimp in a bowl of ice cubes to stop the cooking process. Transfer the shrimp to a fresh bowl and refrigerate until ready to serve.

Serve with tomato dill or creamy dill dip.

Tomato Dill Dip

3 tablespoons	45 ml	mayonnaise
2 tablespoons	30 ml	tomato paste
1 teaspoon	5 ml	Worcestershire sauce
3 tablespoons	45 ml	chopped fresh dill
1 tablespoon	15 ml	freshly squeezed lemon juice
¼ teaspoon	1.25 ml	salt
1 teaspoon	5 ml	hot sauce

In a small bowl, combine the mayonnaise, tomato paste, Worcestershire sauce, chopped dill, lemon juice, salt, and hot sauce.

Refrigerate until ready to serve.

Creamy Dill Dip

4 tablespoons	60 ml	soft, light cream cheese spread
3 tablespoons	45 ml	mayonnaise
1 tablespoon	15 ml	finely chopped fresh dill
¼ teaspoon	1.25 ml	lemon-and-pepper seasoning

In a small bowl, combine the cream cheese, mayonnaise, dill, and seasoning. Stir with a spatula until well blended.

Refrigerate until ready to serve.

Potatoes Make Paint—
Good Soup, Too

The potato has been circling the globe for a long time. It traveled from North America to Europe with the Spanish explorers in the 1500s. From there it toured England, Ireland, and eventually Scotland. It returned to North America with the British in the early 1600s.

The modern Prince Edward Island potato industry produces seed potatoes, fresh table potatoes, processed potatoes in the form of French fries, potato chips, dehydrated potatoes, canned potatoes, and potato flour. A potato contains about the same amount of calories as a banana, apple, or orange and offers more dietary fiber than cabbage or cucumbers. It is a low-salt-content vegetable. Potatoes are found in alcoholic drinks, custard powders, and ice cream. They play a part in the skin care, pharmaceutical, textile, and paint industries, as well as the manufacture of acetone, adhesives, and plastics. The versatility of potato by-products is as surprising as the giant potato that stands outside the Potato Museum in O'Leary, P.E.I.

After five weeks on Prince Edward Island, there was no doubt that we would create a potato recipe. This is our all-time favorite.

Cream of Potato Soup

(Serves 6 to 8)

4	4	medium to large potatoes
2 tablespoons	30 ml	butter
1 cup	240 ml	finely diced onion
4 cups	960 ml	water
2	2	large chicken bouillon cubes
2	2	large bay leaves
3 tablespoons	45 ml	cornstarch
6 tablespoons	90 ml	water
½ teaspoon	2.5 ml	salt
¼ teaspoon	1.25 ml	coarse black pepper
1 cup	240 ml	whipping cream
2 tablespoons	30 ml	chopped fresh parsley

Thinly peel the potatoes, cut them in quarters, and place them in a saucepan with enough water to cover. Boil until the potatoes are soft and falling apart.

Remove the potatoes from the heat. Do not drain. Mash them in their water with either a masher or a hand mixer. The result will be the texture of smooth applesauce.

In a large saucepan, melt the butter and add the onion. Stir constantly over medium heat until the onion is translucent.

Add the water and the bouillon cubes to the diced onions. Stir until the bouillon cubes are dissolved. Add the bay leaves and the mashed potatoes. Stir until the contents are thoroughly combined then bring them to a boil. Keep at a low boil for 15 minutes.

Combine the cornstarch and the water in a small bowl until the mixture is smooth. Slowly add the cornstarch to the soup pot, stirring constantly. Cook on medium heat for 5 minutes.

Remove the bay leaves. Add the salt, pepper, and cream. Heat for 2 or 3 more minutes and serve. Garnish each bowl with a sprinkle of chopped fresh parsley.

Making a Good Thing Better

Vancouver Island is 312 miles (502 kilometers) long. Victoria, the capital of British Columbia, is on the island. Towns like Duncan, Parksville, Sydney, Sooke, Tofino, Ucluelet, Nanaimo, Chemainus, Port Hardy, and their surrounding areas offer totem poles, beaches, whales, kayaks, gardens, museums, murals, lighthouses, native art, birds, restaurants, ancient forests, hiking trails, marinas, guaranteed successful fishing, and more. The island is an eclectic combination of culture, nature, and adventure.

Often, people take something good and turn it into something better. This could be said for Chemainus. A downtown revitalization program turned Chemainus into a work of art. Internationally known artists created the world's largest outdoor art gallery. There are murals everywhere. Local homeowners and business owners who believed that history was too important to be forgotten offered their exterior house and shop walls as canvases for the murals that depict actual historical events.

One mural that intrigued us was the "Telephone Exchange." We had to look closely to determine if the bicycle leaning against the front porch was part of the painting. Just off the main highway that runs between Victoria and Nanaimo, the "Native Heritage" mural stands like a giant postcard at the entrance to town.

The flavors in this leek and potato soup make a good thing better, too.

Leek and Potato Soup

(Serves 4)

4	4	large potatoes, cut in 1-inch cubes
1 cup	240 ml	chopped leeks, white part only
4	4	slices bacon, cut into small squares
4 cups	960 ml	water
1	1	bay leaf
1	1	chicken bouillon cube
½ teaspoon	2.5 ml	black pepper
1 ¼ cups	420 ml	table cream
3 tablespoons	45 ml	cider vinegar

Cover the potato cubes with water to keep them from turning brown.

The interlocking leaves of the leeks tend to catch large amounts of sand and grit. Whether picked in the wild or in a grocery store, they need to be thoroughly rinsed under running water. It's best to trim away the tough green portions. The white inner circles are the best part.

In a large soup pot, sauté the chopped bacon and chopped leeks. Stir over medium-low heat for about 4 minutes.

Add the 4 cups water to the soup pot. Drain the cubed potatoes and add them to the soup pot.

Break the bay leaf in half and put both halves into the pot. Cook over medium heat for about 20 minutes, or until the potatoes are soft.

Add the chicken bouillon cube and pepper. Stir to dissolve the bouillon cube and cook for 5 minutes more. If the potatoes are not broken up, mash them with a fork.

Stir in the table cream.

Bring the soup back to a slow boil. Stir in the cider vinegar.

Remove the bay leaves before serving. If the soup is too thick, add more water or cream 1 tablespoon at a time. Ladle into bowls and serve.

Nostalgia at Jukebox Heaven

Even after touring around the Rio Grande Valley of Texas for over two months, we still stumbled upon interesting, out-of-the-way jewels. Take Smitty's Juke Box Museum, for example. It is a part of Smitty's Music and Amusement on State Street in Pharr, across the street from two railway cars decorated with graffiti. The railway cars are going nowhere on tracks that haven't been used for years.

Smitty's dusty front windows are filled with old phonographs, cigarette machines, and jukeboxes that haven't yet experienced his rejuvenating touch. Inside, past the guest book, the room is crammed with gems from the past. A 1942 Wurlitzer is playing a scratchy, muffled version of "Sentimental Journey" on a seventy-eight, while etchings of deer and fruit on the glass front panels change color with the music.

Smitty's son, Junior, took a quarter out of the front pocket of his tight jeans that snuggled down over his cowboy boots and slipped it into the slot of a 1929 Electramuse. We stood and smiled to "South of the Border" sung by a voice that sounded a lot like Gene Autry. Just stepping into the room makes a baby boomer feel good.

Junior's mother remained behind the office window, barely visible through all the newspaper clippings, photos, and letters describing her late-husband's jukebox collection and love of music.

Jukebox-florescent lime and orange are predominant shades at Smitty's. It's a strange combination of colors, but it delights the senses, just like the lime and carrot in this soup.

Lime and Carrot Soup

(Serves 2 or 3)

1 tablespoon	15 ml	margarine
1 teaspoon	5 ml	finely chopped ginger root
2	2	cloves garlic, finely chopped
½ cup	120 ml	finely chopped onion
3 cups	720 ml	chicken broth
¾ cup	180 ml	uncooked egg noodles
1½ cups	360 ml	thinly sliced baby carrots
2 tablespoons	30 ml	fresh lime juice

Melt the margarine in a saucepan over medium heat. Add the ginger, garlic, and onion. Stir and cook for 2 minutes.

Add the chicken broth and turn the heat to medium-high.

Break the egg noodles into bite-sized pieces.

Stir in the egg noodles, sliced baby carrots, and fresh lime juice.

Cook for 12 to 15 minutes, until the carrots and noodles are tender. Stir occasionally. Ladle into bowls and serve.

Nail Soup Hits Hunger on the Head

A woman who lived alone was hungry and had been hungry for a long time. She was weak. She put a pot of water on the stove to boil and fell faint on the floor. The pot boiled dry and rattled so much that the nails in the ceiling vibrated loose and fell into the pot. The woman's neighbors heard the noise and burst into her kitchen. They found her on the floor and the pot of nails on the stove. When they discovered that her cupboards were bare they all ran back to their homes for food. They brought leftovers, fresh produce, and canned goods. It all went into the pot. When the woman was revived and sitting up, the nourishing pot of soup was ready.

The RV world has introduced us to nail soup. At a recent rally, participants were asked to bring an ingredient from their refrigerator or pantry to the Nail Soup Supper. We know that leftovers make the best soup, however, the concept made us a bit anxious. Ingredients that are not planned can produce a pot of disaster. Then again, a pinch of an herb or spice might be all that is required to bring a mixture of flavors together.

Our nail soup recipe was composed of ingredients we had in our motorhome. It required no additional seasoning and was the perfect amount for two, plus a couple of hungry neighbors.

Nail Soup

(Serves 4)

¼ cup	60 ml	canned mushrooms
10 ounces	300 ml	chicken broth
19 ounces	570 ml	canned diced tomatoes
¾ cup	180 ml	sliced carrots
¾ cup	180 ml	diced celery
16	16	cocktail-size frozen cooked meatballs
14 ounces	420 ml	canned green beans, drained
1	1	beef bouillon cube
1 cup	240 ml	cooked pasta (optional)
½ cup	120 ml	shredded cheddar cheese
4 teaspoons	20 ml	light sour cream

Put the mushrooms, chicken broth, and diced tomatoes into a saucepan.

Heat to a slow boil and add the carrots, celery, frozen meatballs, and green beans.

Add the bouillon cube and stir well to dissolve the cube. Cook for 15 minutes.

Add the cooked pasta and heat for 3 minutes to warm the pasta.

Place the soup in serving bowls. Top with the cheese and a dollop of sour cream.

Beer Cheese Soup Is Something to Bleat About

A fresh seafood market and restaurant named Goatfeathers, in Santa Rosa Beach, Florida, has a sign outside the door that defines "goat feathers" as, "the distractions, sidelines, and deflections that take a man's attention from his business and keep him from getting ahead." It is a quotation from Ellis Parker Butler, cited from 1913. The owners use the sign to attract attention to their premises.

Fresh grouper, pompano, trigger fish, crawfish, crab, amberjack, flounder, and Florida lobster nestle in chipped ice in the lower level seafood market. The beer cheese soup is one of the biggest sellers in the restaurant upstairs. We ordered it not only because it was a distraction and a sideline from the predominantly seafood menu, but also because we were intrigued by the beer-and-cheese combination.

Unless you have a food processor, this recipe requires a lot of chopping. Too much chopping? Horse feathers, or rather, goatfeathers! The flavor is worth it.

Spicy Beer Cheese Soup

(Serves 8 to 10)

1	1	stalk celery
1	1	green pepper
⅓	⅓	Spanish onion
2	2	carrots
2	2	cloves garlic
1	1	red pepper
¼ pound	113 g	bacon
2 cups	480 ml	mild nacho cheese sauce or cheez whiz
2	2	chicken bouillon cubes
2 cups	480 ml	skim milk, whole milk, half-and-half, or cream
¼ cup	60 ml	hot sauce
8 ounces	240 ml	beer

Finely chop the celery, green pepper, onion, carrots, garlic, and red pepper.

Dice the bacon and place it in a soup pot over medium-high heat. Stir for 1 minute to get it sizzling, then add the chopped celery, green peppers, onion, carrots, garlic, and red pepper. Continue to cook and stir until the vegetables are tender.

Turn down the heat to medium and add the cheese sauce and bouillon cubes. Stir until the cubes are dissolved.

Add the milk and hot sauce and stir well in order to blend all the ingredients.

Pour in the beer, stir thoroughly, and simmer for approximately 15 minutes. Ladle into bowls and serve.

If You Don't Grow It, You Have to Mine It

Ron Jung, Mill Supervisor at the Golden Giant Mine in Northern Ontario, had a sign above his desk that said, "If you don't grow it, you have to mine it." The words were a direct quote from his father, who was also a miner.

"Think of any luxury," Ron told us. "Pens. Bedsprings. Automobiles. All these things have one thing in common: they are products created from mined materials."

The Golden Giant Mine is on the appropriately named Yellow Brick Road between Marathon and Wawa off Highway 17 above Lake Superior. In the Golden Giant Mine there are very few large gold nuggets. Instead, gold particles are scattered throughout the rocks. There are only about ten milligrams of gold per ton of ore. To extract the gold, ore-laden rocks that are the size of busses are reduced down to granules the size and texture of chocolate pudding. At the final stage, when the gold is separated from any remaining ore, it is heated and poured into bricks. The mine produces one 66-pound (30-kilogram) gold brick per day.

The Golden Giant had been open for seventeen years. Mining is a finite job. When the gold is completely harvested, the mine closes down. When we visited, the Golden Giant Mine was scheduled to shut down in four years. Graders, jeeps, trucks, and machine parts that were used underground will remain in the mineshafts, buried forever. The miners move on to another site.

This golden sweet potato soup is as good as gold.

Chilled Sweet Potato Soup

(Serves 2)

1	1	large sweet potato
2 tablespoons	30 ml	diced onion
1¼ cups	300 ml	chicken broth
3 ounces	90 ml	whipping cream
½ teaspoon	2.5 ml	ground cardamom
		salt and pepper

Peel and dice the sweet potato. Dice the onion. Combine the sweet potato, diced onion, and chicken broth in a saucepan. Cook on medium heat until the onion and sweet potato are tender.

Place the mixture in a blender and purée until smooth. Transfer the mixture to a bowl. Set it in the refrigerator to chill.

Add the whipping cream and ground cardamom to the chilled soup. Taste the soup. Add salt and pepper to taste. Whisk the ingredients until they are well mixed. Return the soup to the refrigerator to chill the cream.

This is a thick soup but if it needs a little thinning add more cream or water or both. Ladle the chilled sweet potato soup into serving bowls and trickle a thin line of whipping cream on top as garnish.

Christmas Morning in Nuevo Progreso

On December 25, 2002, we spent a Christmas Day like no other and experienced the true meaning of gift giving. We were fortunate to tag along with the Amigos de Los Ninos de Mexico, "Friends of the Children of Mexico," a volunteer group of Americans and Canadians who spend their winters in the Rio Grande Valley of Texas. Every year these Winter Texans gather food and toys for the children in the Nuevo Progreso area of Mexico. Nuevo Progreso is a border town across the Rio Grande River from Texas.

Early Christmas morning, three thousand Mexican children arrived in the town from outlying areas where homes are unheated, where makeshift dwellings have leaky roofs and children sleep side by side on wood and dirt floors. For several hours, the children waited patiently and quietly in a mile-long line around the chain-link fence of the Nuevo Progreso schoolyard. There was no pushing, yelling, or crying. Many were accompanied by mothers, fathers, grandmothers, or an older sibling.

At ten o'clock, a parade of Winter Texans gathered on the Mexican side of the border and marched several blocks down the main street to the schoolyard. Santa and Mrs. Claus followed in a wagon pulled by a donkey.

Volunteers were stationed along both sides of long tables filled with apples, oranges, bananas, wieners rolled in flour tortillas, potato chips, packaged cupcakes, cookies, bundles of Hershey kisses, candies, boxed juices, pencils, toys, and teddy bears. Each child received a plastic grocery bag and then proceeded single file along the food and gift line. At the end of the line, the children shook hands with Santa and Mrs. Claus. The smiles on the children's faces made this a Christmas we will never forget.

Tortilla Soup

(Serves 2)

2 tablespoons	30 ml	butter
½	½	medium onion, finely chopped
2	2	cloves garlic, finely chopped
1	1	stalk celery, chopped
2 cups	480 ml	chicken broth
1 cup	240 ml	water
1	1	medium carrot, cut in rounds
¼	¼	green zucchini, diced
¼	¼	yellow zucchini, diced
½	½	medium potato, diced
½	½	red pepper, diced
¼	¼	green pepper, diced
1	1	jalapeño pepper, seeds removed, thinly sliced
1 cup	240 ml	cubed cooked chicken
4 to 6	4 to 6	dashes hot sauce
3 tablespoons	45 ml	coarsely chopped fresh cilantro
2	2	flour tortillas

In a saucepan over medium heat, combine the butter, onion, garlic, and celery. Stir until the onion is translucent.

Add the chicken broth, water, carrot, green zucchini, yellow zucchini, potato, red pepper, green pepper, jalapeño pepper, chicken, hot sauce, and cilantro. Cook until the vegetables are tender. While the soup is cooking, prepare the tortilla topping.

Cut 2 flour tortillas in quarters and then into 1-inch-long, ¼-inch-wide strips.

Heat a nonstick frying pan over medium-high heat. Spread the tortilla strips around the bottom of the frying pan. Lightly brown and turn the tortilla strips often in the frying pan until crisp but not burnt.

Ladle the soup into bowls and top with tortilla strips.

This Soup Is Made to Be Shared

"Have people been friendly to you? Why don't you come taste our soup?"

Guy Tremblay approached us in a campground in an area of Quebec that we had been told was separatist country. Several days before, we learned that "gourganes" were the special beans that people in this Lac St. Jean area of Quebec use to make soup. We joined Guy and the hundred other members of the Club de Camping et Caravaning Saguenay around their soup pot. We met the directors of the club and Madame "Chef" and her husband as they used a wooden spoon the size of a paddle to stir the contents of the huge pot. Cobs of corn bobbed in the bubbling broth.

Guy and his friends not only shared friendship with us, they gave us a list of the basic ingredients of their bean soup. We were also given plaques that make us honorary members of their camping club. A big pot of this Saguenay bean soup in anyone's backyard is sure to entice the whole neighborhood.

Saguenay Bean Soup

(Serves 8 to 10)

2 ¾ cups	660 ml	large dried lima beans
5	5	cobs of corn
1 pound	454 g	bacon, chopped small
2 cups	480 ml	diced onion
15 cups	3.6 L	water
1 ½ cups	360 ml	carrots, cut in thin rounds
¾ cup	180 ml	barley
½ teaspoon	2.5 ml	summer savory
1 teaspoon	5 ml	salt
½ teaspoon	2.5 ml	black pepper

Rinse the beans. In order to soften the beans quickly, place them in a saucepan. Boil water in a kettle and pour it over the beans. Let the beans sit for 3 or 4 minutes. Drain them and set them aside.

Peel the corn cobs and trim the ends. Cut each cob in half.

Place the chopped bacon and diced onion in a deep soup pot and stir over medium heat until the onions are translucent. The bacon will be soft and steaming.

Add the water to the pot and stir. Add the carrot slices, beans, corn, and barley.

Bring the mixture to a boil and then simmer for 1½ hours, or until the beans are tender. Stir occasionally to prevent sticking.

About 10 minutes before serving, add the summer savory, salt, and pepper. Remove the corncobs and serve them as a side dish with the soup. Ladle the soup into bowls and serve.

Aloe Vera Is Optional in This Salad

At the one-hundred-acre Southern Fields Aloe Farm in Weslaco, Texas, we learned the process of hand-harvesting aloe vera as well as the plant's many benefits.

Standing between the perfect rows of two-foot high plants, J. R. Sigrist removed a leaf and used his pocketknife to skin it and produce a slippery aloe fillet. He explained that if the gel is put on a scraped knee, and the scrape isn't washed, the gel will heal the wound with the dirt inside.

"Aloe vera gel has a healing effect on warts, hemorrhoids, heel spurs, seed corns, and burns. Add it to the bean pot to eliminate embarrassing gas and place it in marinades to tenderize meat. Rub it in your hair, let it stand for an hour, and then rinse, and your hair will be soft, smooth, and full of protein. When consumed as a juice or chopped in a salad it is believed to be good for the digestive tract and high blood pressure," said Audrey Sigrist, who owns and operates the farm with her husband, J. R.

Small cubes of aloe vera are optional in the following salad.

Avocado, Shrimp, and Orange Salad

(Serves 2 or 3)

8	8	cloves garlic, quartered
2 teaspoons	10 ml	canola oil
16 to 18	16 to 18	cooked large shrimp
3 tablespoons	45 ml	fresh lemon juice
¼ teaspoon	1.25 ml	salt
¼ teaspoon	1.25 ml	pepper
2	2	navel oranges, cut into sections
2	2	ripe avocados
1	1	head leaf lettuce, broken into bite-sized pieces
3 ounces	90 ml	red onion, thinly sliced
10	10	green olives, cut into quarters
½	½	jalapeño pepper, finely chopped
1 tablespoon	15 ml	chopped fresh cilantro or parsley
4 tablespoons	60 ml	balsamic vinegar
6 tablespoons	90 ml	extra virgin olive oil

In a frying pan, cook and stir the garlic quarters in the canola oil over medium heat for 3 minutes, or until the garlic is tender. Add the cooked shrimp, lemon juice, salt, and pepper. Stir and cook for 1 minute. Remove from the heat.

With a sharp, thin-bladed knife cut off both ends of the orange. Place the orange on a cutting board with the flat end down. Cut away the peel from top to bottom along the curvature of the fruit, removing all the white pulp from the orange. Hold the peeled orange in one hand and cut down along both membranes of a section to the center then turn the knife to loosen the section and lift it out. Remove other sections in the same way.

Peel the avocadoes and cut them in half lengthwise. Remove the pit and cut the avocado into ¼-inch-thick slices.

Place the lettuce on individual salad plates.

In a bowl, toss the onion slices, olive pieces, chopped jalapeños, and chopped cilantro with the cooked shrimp and garlic pieces.

Place the shrimp mixture in the center of the lettuce plates.

Arrange the orange and avocado slices around the edge of the plates.

Combine the balsamic vinegar and olive oil. Mix thoroughly, then trickle the dressing over the lettuce and shrimp.

Manatees Love Salads

The natural plant diet of the Florida Manatee sounds interesting enough to be on the salad menu at a trendy café. Water lettuce. Turtle grass. Eurasian watermilfoil. Water hyacinth. Florida elodea.

The average manatee weighs about one thousand pounds and is approximately ten feet long. They can live in fresh, brackish, or salt water. Water temperatures below 68°F (20°C) are intolerable for them, so in the winter they roam the warm waterways of Florida and southern Georgia. The mammal has a seal-like body that tapers to a flat, paddle-shaped tail. Two small forelimbs on its upper body have three to four nails on each flipper. Its large head and face are wrinkled, and its snout has stiff whiskers. Florida law protects the manatees. Boaters, divers, and swimmers are warned not to frighten, touch, or disturb the non-aggressive, reclusive creatures.

Manatees spend most of their time eating. They graze along water bottoms as well as at the surface. They are agile, playful, harmless creatures without natural enemies. If left alone by humans they live a simple, shy, contented life without designated territories or group politics. When traditional floating plants and grasses are not available they are quite content to munch on other forms of vegetation, including salad greens.

Garlicky Balsamic Chicken Caesar

(Serves 2 or 3)

4 or 5	4 or 5	large cloves garlic, minced
2 tablespoons	30 ml	fresh lemon juice
2 tablespoons	30 ml	balsamic vinegar
1 teaspoon	5 ml	Worcestershire sauce
½ teaspoon	2.5 ml	dry mustard
¼ teaspoon	1.25 ml	coarse ground pepper
4 tablespoons	60 ml	extra virgin olive oil
2	2	boneless, skinless chicken breasts
½ teaspoon	2.5 ml	coarse ground pepper
		olive oil cooking spray
1	1	head romaine lettuce
		Parmesan cheese, grated
½	½	lemon, cut in wedges

In a large measuring cup or deep bowl, whisk to blend the minced garlic, lemon juice, balsamic vinegar, Worcestershire sauce, mustard, and pepper. Put the olive oil in last and add slowly while whisking vigorously.

Cut each chicken breast into 8 strips lengthwise. Pat the chicken strips dry with a paper towel and place them on a plate. Sprinkle the chicken strips with coarse ground pepper.

Spray a frying pan with olive oil cooking spray. Fry the chicken strips over medium-high heat for about 5 minutes, or until the chicken is cooked through and brown on the outside.

Break the romaine into bite-sized pieces. Pour the dressing over the romaine and toss well to coat the leaves.

Sprinkle the salad with grated Parmesan cheese. Garnish the top of the salad with the chicken strips and lemon wedges.

Déjà Vu at the New Perry Hotel

The New Perry Hotel, in Perry, Georgia, was built in 1925. We discovered it by accident several years ago when we pulled off I-75 for something to eat. We rediscovered it on our way to a large RV rally in Perry. The minute we walked into the lobby of the hotel, we knew we had been there before. We sat at the same table and thought even the diners next to us looked familiar.

Travelers have rested and eaten at the old Perry Hotel ever since it was built in 1870. The good old-fashioned southern cooking has remained consistent. The after-church and tourist clientele choose from baked sugar-cured ham, fried chicken, chicken pie, salmon croquettes, Spanish mackerel, fillet of perch, broiled chopped steak, roast turkey, or lamb, with corn, beans, yams, turnip greens, soup, and congealed salad. Management boasts that more than 80 percent of their diners have eaten at the hotel before.

We have added rhubarb to our version of the New Perry Hotel's strawberry congealed side salad. The New Perry Hotel Coffee Shop garnishes their salad with a dollop of mayonnaise.

Strawberry-Rhubarb Congealed Salad

(Serves 10)

5 ounces	142 g	frozen strawberries
5 ounces	142 g	frozen rhubarb
6.5 ounces	195 ml	canned crushed pineapple, drained
1	1	banana, sliced
3 ounces	85 g	strawberry Jell-O powder
1 cup	240 ml	boiling water
½ cup	120 ml	light sour cream

Blend the frozen strawberries, frozen rhubarb, pineapple, and banana in a blender until smooth. Combine in a large bowl and set aside.

Dissolve the strawberry Jell-O in the boiling water, stirring until completely dissolved.

Add the strawberry, rhubarb, banana, and pineapple mixture to the hot Jell-O and stir until thawed and thoroughly blended.

Pour one half of the mixture into a serving bowl and chill for about 30 minutes, until partially set. Keep the remaining half of the mixture at room temperature.

Spread the sour cream evenly over the chilled, partially-set mixture.

Spoon the remaining room-temperature mixture over the sour cream and chill until firm.

A History Lesson from the Road

Coteau-du-Lac is a small town along the shore of the St. Lawrence River, southwest of Montreal, Quebec. In the 1750s, the nearby rapids were a detriment to anyone who wanted access to the Great Lakes in a boat larger than a canoe. French navigators dug a narrow canal through the rocks along the river's edge. This enabled traders, explorers, and adventurers to pull their wooden boats, loaded with supplies, around the rapids.

In 1779, the British expanded the system by digging a lock canal. They feared an invasion from the Americans to the south. By the time the war of 1812 was underway, a fort was in place to defend the canal.

At the National Historic Site at Coteau-du-Lac we walked along the shore of the St. Lawrence, looked down into the original stone-carved canal, and studied the remains of the lock canal, the first in North America and the forerunner of the St. Lawrence Seaway.

Antique cannons point across the river, standing guard over a bit of history that we happened upon by accident. We never know when a turn in the road will provide a new lesson. This recipe provides a new way to enjoy French-style green beans.

French-Style Green Bean Salad

(Serves 4 or 5)

4 cups	960 ml	frozen French-style green beans
⅓ cup	80 ml	canola oil
¾ cup	180 ml	cider vinegar
4 tablespoons	60 ml	sugar
¾ teaspoon	3.75 ml	salt
½ teaspoon	2.5 ml	black pepper
2 tablespoons	30 ml	finely chopped onion

Cook the frozen French-style beans in as little water as possible until the ice is gone. The beans should remain bright green and firm.

Drain the beans in a colander. Run cold water over the beans to prevent further cooking.

Combine the oil, vinegar, sugar, salt, pepper, and chopped onion in a bowl. Mix well.

Add the dressing to the beans. Mix thoroughly and refrigerate until serving.

A Souvenir from Manitoba

We got our first windshield chip in Manitoba. The motorhome was less than three months old. We had driven through several miles of construction on the Trans Canada Highway around Lake Superior without any problems. As soon as we entered Manitoba's four-lane super highway, a little car passed us and threw a stone. It is one of our souvenirs of Manitoba.

After a family reunion in Winnipeg, we took a side trip north to Dauphin, where Lamont's mother was born. Lamont's grandfather was a doctor in Dauphin in the early 1900s.

The town lies in a fertile valley. Flat farm fields spread away from both sides of the main highway. This terrain is similar to the homeland steppes of the Eastern European immigrants who helped to establish Dauphin in the late 1800s.

Every year, mid-summer, Dauphin becomes engulfed in the colors, music, and food of the National Ukrainian Festival. Floral headdresses, embroidered blouses, swirling skirts, energetic music, and traditional Ukrainian food entice visitors from around the world.

A wooden palisade designed after a fur-trading fort of the North West Company surrounds the Fort Dauphin Museum. A trapper's cabin, schoolhouse, church, blacksmith shop, trading post, and pioneer house are furnished in the style of the early settlers.

Lentils are native to the Old World. Because they have an earthy flavor, they require accompanying flavors to make them exciting. Their high nutritional value makes them worth the effort. Lamont's grandfather would likely approve of this healthy salad.

Refreshing Lentil Salad

(Serves 8)

1 cup	240 ml	green lentils
		grated zest of 1 lemon
½ cup	120 ml	oil-cured black olives
1	1	small, firm mango
2 tablespoons	30 ml	capers
¼ cup	60 ml	chopped fresh oregano
2	2	cloves garlic, chopped
¼ cup	60 ml	chopped fresh parsley
1 tablespoon	15 ml	lemon juice
1 pinch	1 pinch	salt
1 pinch	1 pinch	pepper
1 tablespoon	15 ml	extra virgin olive oil

Rinse the lentils thoroughly and place them in a saucepan. Cover them with at least 2 inches of cold water. Add the lemon zest and bring the contents to a boil. Cover the saucepan and simmer for 30 minutes. While the lentils simmer, prepare the other ingredients.

Drain the lentils and set them aside.

Squeeze the black olives in order to remove the pits. Either break or chop the olive flesh into thirds.

The olives will leave a black stain, so wash your hands and cutting board immediately.

Dice the flesh of the mango.

Combine the olive pieces, capers, oregano, garlic, parsley, and lentils. Sprinkle the diced mango over the mixture.

Mix the lemon juice, olive oil, salt, and pepper in a small jar and shake well. Drizzle the dressing over the salad.

Northern Hospitality

Inuvik in the Northwest Territories has a population of three thousand two hundred. It is home to the Igloo Church and the Great Northern Arts Festival. The community is unique because of its adaptation to the northern climate. Inuvik's buildings sit on pilings in order to protect the permafrost below. Utilities are encased above ground in utilidors. Shoes are removed at the entrance to the library. Children read in stocking feet, under the watchful eye of a large polar bear skin. An arena is converted into a community greenhouse. A hotel menu offers musk ox pot roast. Fireworks are out of the question on July 1, Canada Day, because they require darkness. In the far north, every year beginning on June 21, there are twenty-four hours of daylight for six weeks.

During our first day in Inuvik, we took a tour with Regional Tourism Officer Judith Venaas. She invited us to dinner and gave us a gift of low-bush cranberries that she had picked at the Arctic Circle.

Cranberry, Brie, and Scallop Salad

(Serves 2)

3 tablespoons	45 ml	sweetened, dried cranberries
3 tablespoons	45 ml	cranberry juice cocktail
2 tablespoons	30 ml	balsamic vinegar
2 tablespoons	30 ml	extra virgin olive oil
½ teaspoon	2.5 ml	coarse ground black pepper
		baby lettuce greens
1	1	ripe pear
1 tablespoon	15 ml	fresh lemon juice
3.5 ounces	100 g	double-cream Brie cheese
20	20	bay scallops
1 teaspoon	5 ml	extra virgin olive oil

Make the cranberry dressing several hours ahead to allow the flavors to blend. Stir the dried cranberries, cranberry juice, balsamic vinegar, olive oil, and black pepper together. Refrigerate until ready to use.

Cover the bottom of individual dinner plates with lettuce pieces.

Cut the pear in half and remove the core. Cut each half of the pear into 6 to 8 lengthwise slices. Place the pear slices into a bowl and coat them gently with lemon juice to prevent them from turning brown.

Remove any excess lemon juice with a paper towel and fan the pear slices on top of the lettuce along one side of each of the plates.

Cut the cheese wedge in half and place a half-wedge on the lettuce along one side of each plate.

Rinse the scallops and pat dry.

Heat the oil over medium-high heat in a non-stick frying pan. Add the scallops to the hot oil.

Cook the small bay scallops for 1 minute. Remove them immediately to prevent over cooking.

Arrange the warm scallops on top of the lettuce on the remaining third of each plate. Spoon the cranberry dressing over the scallops, Brie, and pear slices.

Seeking Seashells by the Seashore

Numerous islands off the Gulf Coast of Florida offer a myriad of water activities and experiences. Boating. Sunbathing. Quiet moments at dusk or dawn on deserted docks. Seashelling.

The girl of our childhood tongue twister—the one who sold seashells by the seashore—probably suffered from what is known as the Sanibel Stoop. This is the shell-bent stance of island shellers as they stoop to pick through the shells provided by the latest storm or washed ashore by the early morning tide. Walking along the beach of Sanibel and Captiva Islands in southwest Florida, like everyone who has ever strolled at water's edge, we, too, did the stoop.

Cockles and conchs are common on Sanibel. Shellers who find the more coveted junonia shell get their pictures in the local newspaper. The junonia shell looks much like a brown-spotted version of the pasta shells of the following recipe.

Shell Pasta Salad

(Serves 4 to 6)

3 cups	720 ml	uncooked large shell pasta
½ cup	120 ml	mayonnaise
2 tablespoons	30 ml	Dijon mustard
2 tablespoons	30 ml	lemon juice
2 tablespoons	30 ml	red wine vinegar
½ cup	120 ml	olive oil
2	2	large cloves garlic, finely chopped
½ teaspoon	2.5 ml	black pepper
1 ½ teaspoons	7.5 ml	salt
½ cup	120 ml	chopped green onions
2	2	roma tomatoes, diced small
¼ pound	114 g	feta cheese, crumbled
¼ cup	60 ml	finely chopped fresh parsley
12	12	kalamata olives

Cook the pasta shells in boiling water until they are cooked but still firm. Don't overcook. Stir gently and frequently to prevent the shells from sticking to the bottom of the pot.

Put the cooked shells into a sieve and rinse under cold water.

Combine the mayonnaise, mustard, lemon juice, wine vinegar, olive oil, garlic, pepper, and salt in a bowl or measuring cup.

In a large bowl, combine the mayonnaise mixture and the pasta shells. Stir gently to coat the pasta.

Gently stir in the chopped green onions and tomatoes.

Sprinkle the feta cheese and parsley over top. Garnish with the olives.

Golfing in the Land of the Midnight Sun

A lmost three-quarters of the thirty thousand people living in the Yukon Territory live in Whitehorse. For such a small population, Whitehorse is a full-facility town. It offers an arts center, a full-service college, and the Territorial Archives.

In late August, our tee-off time at the Mountain View Golf Course in Whitehorse was seven in the evening. There was no need for fluorescent golf balls or a flashlight. The fairways were like well-kept lawns. This condition was unique for a golf course located in the sub-arctic climate north of the sixtieth parallel of latitude that marks the northern borders of British Columbia, Alberta, Saskatchewan, and Manitoba.

The Mountain View Golf Course is located just off the Alaska Highway on Skookum Road. Set in the Yukon River Valley, all eighteen holes are on the bluff above the river. Because of its location in the Land of the Midnight Sun, with virtually twenty-four hours of sunlight in peak summer, a golfer can tee off in bright sunlight as early as 6:30 in the morning or as late as 9:00 at night.

Sunshine Salad

(Serves 2)

½	½	navel orange
2 tablespoons	30 ml	white sugar
1 tablespoon	15 ml	water
16	16	pecan halves
1 tablespoon	15 ml	orange juice
1 tablespoon	15 ml	grapefruit juice
1 tablespoon	15 ml	balsamic vinegar
½ teaspoon	2.5 ml	soy sauce
⅛ teaspoon	0.63 ml	salt
⅛ teaspoon	0.63 ml	pepper
1 tablespoon	15 ml	canola oil
½	½	head lettuce
4	4	romaine lettuce leaves
4	4	thinly cut red onion rings

Cut the orange in half lengthwise, not across the middle. Cut each half into quarters. Using a sharp knife, cut along the edge of the flesh removing the peel and white pulp. Place the flesh on a cutting board. Gently slice each piece in half crosswise.

In a small nonstick frying pan, combine the sugar and water and bring the liquid to a boil. Cook and stir the liquid for 5 minutes.

Add the pecan halves to the hot sugar water. Coat the pecans with the liquid and continue to stir until the syrup turns to a white, sugary coating on the pecans. This will happen quickly, so be prepared to remove the pecans to a plate. Set the candied nuts aside to cool and dry.

Make the vinaigrette by combining the orange juice, grapefruit juice, balsamic vinegar, soy sauce, salt, pepper, and canola oil in a bowl. Set aside.

Break up and combine the head lettuce and romaine leaves. Arrange the lettuce blend in the center of each salad plate. Cut the onion rings in half and place them in the center of the lettuce. Place 4 orange pieces around the outside of the lettuce and place 2 candied pecans in the spaces between the orange pieces.

Whisk the vinaigrette one more time and trickle it evenly over the contents of the salad. Any leftover dressing may solidify when refrigerated, so bring it to room temperature and whisk vigorously before using.

Fall Asleep and the Kudzu Will Get You

Kudzu grows so quickly in the southeastern United States that people chop it down to prevent it from covering fences, buildings, trees, and television antennae. In winter, the gray, beige, leafless vine lies dormant, draped in scary shapes along the roadsides. In the hot weather, the leafy green plant can creep one hundred feet in a single season, obsessed with rooting wherever its leaves touch the earth. In Atlanta, the story is that if you set yourself up in a lawn chair, the kudzu will grow a foot in front of your eyes. In its quest for space, kudzu has spread its tendrils from Florida to Maryland.

The Japanese introduced the vine to the United States in the nineteenth century. Kudzu quickly became a popular decorative plant in many southern yards. It was an excellent cover for tree stumps and compost piles. It was also used to prevent soil erosion on farms.

Although it is used for food in Japan, we have not created a recipe for kudzu. However, on a tour of the Atlanta area, we enjoyed this delicious apple and bacon sandwich as part of a picnic lunch with friends.

Apple-Bacon Sandwich

(Serves 2)

4 to 6	4 to 6	whole slices bacon
		margarine or butter
		mayonnaise
4	4	slices French bread
		leaf lettuce
4	4	slices golden delicious apple
		nonstick cooking spray
2	2	slices Swiss or white cheddar cheese
¼ cup	60 ml	raisins

Cut the bacon slices in half. Cook the bacon until crisp and drain it on a paper towel.

Spread margarine and mayonnaise on each slice of bread.

Core the apple and cut into ¼-inch slices. Heat a nonstick frying pan to medium-high. Spray the pan with nonstick cooking spray. Cook the apple slices on both sides until browned and tender.

Build each sandwich starting with lettuce, then apple, cheese, raisins, and bacon.

Cut the sandwiches in half and enjoy.

Lobster Is Not the Only Treat on Prince Edward Island

The lobster supper in New Glasgow, Prince Edward Island, is a treat. It starts with fresh rolls hot out of the oven, followed by seafood chowder, steamed cultivated mussels, garden salad, potato salad, and coleslaw. We could have ordered roast beef, ham, or breaded scallops, but we chose to go straight for the lobster. Several bibs, napkins, and wet naps later we had to make choices again. Apple, raisin, cherry, blueberry, or meringue pie. Ice cream, frozen yogurt cream, or strawberry shortcake. Coffee, tea, milk, or soft drink.

Another treat was spending time with Catherine McKinnon who lives on Prince Edward Island part of the year. Catherine's signature song, "Farewell to Nova Scotia," and her regular television appearances on *The Don Messer Show, Singalong Jubilee,* and her own *Catherine McKinnon Show* created pleasure for many of us who are old enough to remember the 1960s. She was a key player in introducing Atlantic Canada's maritime music to the world.

We are thankful that Catherine shared her enthusiasm for Prince Edward Island with us. She also shared the flavors and the idea for this recipe. We first enjoyed the sandwich in Catherine's Spot O'Tea restaurant in Stanley Bridge. It was the fresh basil from Catherine's herb garden that made this sandwich a truly remarkable experience.

Basil-Balsamic Bagel Sandwich

(Serves 4)

8	8	sun-dried tomatoes
½	½	small Spanish onion
1	1	clove garlic
¼ cup	60 ml	balsamic vinegar
¾ cup	180 ml	olive oil
12	12	tomato slices
4 tablespoons	60 ml	feta cheese
12	12	fresh basil leaves
4	4	plain bagels
		olive oil

Place the sun-dried tomatoes in a bowl and cover with boiling water. Set aside for 15 minutes.

Peel the onion and garlic. Cut the onion into large chunks. Cut the garlic cloves in half.

Drain the tomatoes and discard the water. Combine the tomatoes, onion, and garlic in a blender. Blend until the pieces are small.

Add the balsamic vinegar and blend again until the mixture is smooth. Slowly add the olive oil while continuing to blend. Blend for 2 minutes more. Refrigerate the vinaigrette in a covered container. It can be used as a salad dressing as well as a sandwich spread.

Slice the tomatoes, crumble the feta cheese, and wash the basil leaves.

Cut the bagels in half and brush each half with olive oil. Heat a frying pan to medium-high and when the pan is hot, place the bagel halves in the pan oiled side down and toast until they are golden brown.

Place the sliced, toasted bagel open-faced on serving plates. Brush all 8 halves with the balsamic vinaigrette. Cover the bottom halves of each bagel with a generous layer of sliced tomatoes. Top the tomatoes with crumbled feta. Place 2 fresh basil leaves on the feta. Garnish the top half of the open-faced sandwich with a third basil leaf.

A Good Place to Go for Directions

Constructed as a military route to Alaska for U.S. forces in 1942, the Alaska Highway begins at mile "O" in Dawson Creek, B.C., and winds 1,387 miles (2,233 kilometers) north to Delta Junction near Fairbanks, Alaska. It is the most popular route for Americans and Canadians traveling to Alaska and the Yukon.

Watson Lake, Yukon, was an important supply center during construction of the Alaska Highway. It is the first community on the highway, north of the British Columbia–Yukon border. As Canada's "Gateway to the Yukon," Watson Lake is best known for its Signpost Forest that was initiated in 1942 by a homesick American soldier. He was working on the construction of the Alaska Highway and posted a sign pointing the way to his hometown, Danville, Illinois. Since then, people traveling through Watson Lake have posted more than fifty thousand personal messages, license plates, and hometown signs. Detroit, Michigan. Bathurst, New Brunswick. Halifax, Nova Scotia. Tokyo, Japan. Frankfurt, Germany. Cedar Falls, Iowa.

We stayed overnight in Watson Lake. The next morning we discovered that we were parked next door to friends who live in Colorado. They had stopped for one night on their way to Anchorage. We were on our way to Ontario. What a coincidence that our paths crossed at that point on earth, at that particular moment in time. Meeting friends so far from home was even better than finding the names of familiar towns on the signpost.

If direction is needed for a quick lunch with friends, the following recipe might point to it.

Peppered Chicken Wraps

(Serves 6)

3	3	boneless, skinless chicken breasts
		coarse black pepper
1	1	small sweet red pepper
1	1	small cooking onion
1	1	medium portobello mushroom cap
2 tablespoons	30 ml	soy sauce
2 tablespoons	30 ml	lemon juice
1 tablespoon	15 ml	lime juice
2 tablespoons	30 ml	canola oil
6	6	large flour tortillas
6 tablespoons	90 ml	low-fat ranch salad dressing
6	6	lettuce leaves

Trim the fat from the chicken breasts.

Coat one side of each breast generously with coarse black pepper. Gently pound the pepper into the surface of the chicken breast with the blunt edge of a large knife.

Cut the chicken into long thin strips.

Place the peppered chicken strips in a bowl, cover them with plastic wrap, and refrigerate.

Remove the seeds and stem from the red pepper. Cut the pepper into long, thin strips.

Thinly slice the onion and the mushroom cap.

In a large bowl, combine the red pepper, onion, and mushroom strips. In a small bowl combine the soy sauce, lemon juice, and lime juice. Stir the liquid and pour it over the vegetables. Toss until the vegetables are evenly covered with liquid. Set aside.

Heat the oil in a frying pan over medium heat. Cook and stir the chicken strips for 5 minutes, or until cooked.

Add the vegetable mixture and the liquid to the chicken in the frying pan. Stir and cook over medium-high heat for 5 minutes.

Spread 1 tablespoon of salad dressing at the center of each tortilla. Cover the dressing with a leaf of lettuce.

With tongs, lift the chicken and vegetables from the pan into a bowl, leaving the liquid behind.

Place a portion of the chicken and vegetables in the center of each tortilla. Fold the chicken wrap into a package shape for serving.

Simple Is Sometimes Better

Hillsboro, New Mexico, is off the main highway on the Geronimo Trail in the Black Range Mountains. It is small, old, and isolated. The buildings blend in with the rusts and browns of the surrounding hills. Local merchants and neighbors, and any hikers and tourists who are lucky enough to find themselves on the road through town, gather for lunch or coffee at the Hillsboro Café and General Store. According to a local, Hillsboro offers sunshine, no crime, and people who are friendly but mind their own business.

The cemetery is high on a hill overlooking the town. Standing alone among the hundred-year-old crosses, with the wind blowing the dry grass at our feet and the high, barren mountains in the distance, we couldn't help but shed the complications of our daily existence and appreciate how truly simple life is, or should be.

This simple vegetable burger is a variation of the one on the menu at the Hillsboro Café and General Store.

Southwest Veggie Burger

(Serves 2)

2	2	lettuce leaves
4	4	slices of tomato
1	1	medium zucchini
3	3	large mushrooms
1	1	large sweet onion
		Monterey jack cheese
		butter or margarine
2	2	oversized hamburger buns
		nonstick cooking spray
		mild or hot salsa

Place a leaf of lettuce and 2 slices of tomato on the side of each serving plate.

Slice the zucchini into ¼-inch-thick rounds. Cut the mushrooms into ¼-inch-thick slices. Cut the largest part of the onion into 4 large slices, approximately ¼-inch-thick. Thinly slice enough cheese to cover the surface of the hamburger bun.

Butter the insides of the hamburger buns.

Heat a frying pan or griddle to medium-high heat. When the pan is hot, place the hamburger buns in the pan, butter side down. When evenly browned, set the buns, open, on the serving plate.

Spray the hot frying pan with nonstick cooking spray and place the onion slices, mushroom slices, and zucchini slices, into the pan. Brown on both sides.

When the onions, mushrooms, and zucchini are brown and tender, remove them from the heat and layer them on the bottoms of the hamburger buns. Top with the cheese and salsa and serve.

It's Exciting to Meet Someone Who Has Made History

When the men who played professional baseball left the United States for World War II, a group of women known as the All American Girls' Professional Baseball League (AAGPBL) kept the game of major league professional baseball alive.

From its inception in 1943 until the time of its demise in 1954, the AAGPBL included six hundred women recruited from the United States, Canada, and Cuba. Teams like the Rockford Peaches, Milwaukee Chicks, Minneapolis Millerettes, Fort Wayne Daisies, Muskegon Lassies, Springfield Sallies, Battle Creek Belles, and Kalamazoo Lassies drew millions of fans to the stands.

We met Frances Vukovich, who played in the AAGPBL for two years as a Chicago Colleen and a Racine Belle. A rookie pitcher in 1950, she received $3 a day for meals, a free hotel room, and a $55 weekly paycheck.

As a young girl just out of high school, Frances read an ad in a small town Pennsylvania newspaper, threw baseballs at a tryout, and two weeks later received a telegram telling her to report to Indiana for training.

Official recognition came when the girls' league was inducted into the National Baseball Hall of Fame in Cooperstown, New York, in 1988. Annual reunions and a newsletter help the players to keep in touch. Photographs, scorecards, and other AAGPBL paraphernalia are on view at the Northern Indiana Historical Society, in South Bend, Indiana.

"We didn't talk about what we did or know how important it was until the movie, *A League of Their Own*, appeared," Frances said.

This recipe is a winner for both baseball players and fans.

Home-Run Taco Dogs

(Serves 6)

½	½	large green pepper
½	½	large yellow pepper
½	½	large red pepper
½	½	jalapeño pepper
1	1	small onion
1½ tablespoons	22.5 ml	canola oil
6	6	wieners
6	6	hard or soft taco shells
		mustard

Wash, trim, and remove the seeds and membranes from the green, yellow, red, and jalapeño pepper halves. Finely dice the jalapeño pepper and cut the green, yellow, and red peppers into thin strips. Cut the strips in half.

Peel and cut the onion into thin strips.

Place the oil in a deep frying pan and heat to medium-high. Add all the peppers, onion strips, and wieners. Stir until the peppers are tender and the wieners are browned and heated through.

For hard tacos: Place some of the pepper mixture in the bottom of each taco shell. Top the peppers with a wiener. Put mustard on the wieners, then place the remaining peppers over the wieners.

For soft tacos: Place the ingredients at one end and roll the taco into a cigar shape around the filling.

Big, Bold, and Beautiful

The pleasures of Las Vegas stretch beyond the slot machines and glitzy entertainment. The city has become a destination for art lovers. Restaurant walls display the original works of classical artists. Buildings reflect the designs of famous architects.

Dale Chihuly, a Seattle-based glass artist, is famous for his daring pieces. His sculpture of over two thousand individually blown, multicolored glass flowers stretches across the entire ceiling of the lobby of the Bellagio Hotel. The brilliant flowers hang down like a gathering of vibrant umbrellas. Big, bold, and beautiful, the translucent red, green, and yellow oversized petals dance in the Nevada sunlight. As fragrances drift into the lobby from flowers in a nearby conservatory, one can't help but stand in awe with head back and eyes turned to the ceiling.

Just like the glass flowers, this roast beef sandwich is enough to make a hungry person's head turn heavenward.

Big, Bold, and Beautiful Beef Sandwich

(Serves 6)

1 ½ pounds	680 g	cooked roast beef, thinly sliced
⅓ cup	80 ml	Worcestershire sauce
2 tablespoons	30 ml	canola oil
1	1	onion, sliced
1	1	green or yellow pepper, cut into thin strips
		Swiss cheese, sliced
2	2	loaves French bread
		mayonnaise
1	1	tomato, sliced

Place the sliced roast beef in a bowl with the Worcestershire sauce for 15 minutes. Turn the meat several times to coat each slice.

Heat the oil to medium-high in a frying pan. Add the onions and peppers. Cook until the onions and peppers are tender.

Add the roast beef to the frying pan to heat it through.

Slice the loaf of bread in half lengthwise. Butter both sides of the bread.

Heat a frying pan to medium-high. Place each slice of buttered bread into the pan buttered side down. Heat until the bread is a golden brown.

Place the sliced meat on the bottom half of the toasted bread. Cover the meat with the onions and peppers. Spread mayonnaise on the top half of the toasted bread. Cover the mayonnaise with the Swiss cheese. Cover the cheese with the tomato slices. Put the halves of the sandwich together. Cut the sandwich into manageable portions. Serve.

All We Need Is an Inch

Flying J Service Centers are a convenient stop for truckers and RV travelers. At the Flying J we can fill up on fuel and propane, wash the windshield, check all ten tire pressures, empty our holding tanks, fill up with fresh water, and take advantage of free overnight camping. On our way to a destination we often time our stopovers to coincide with Flying J locations.

One particular night, we arrived late to find there was only one spot left in the RV section of a Flying J. At first glance it didn't look as though we would fit. The space appeared to be narrower than our motorhome. From previous parking experience we know that all we need is one spare inch in order to fit.

We inched forward into the space. The driver of one of the other RVs stepped out and offered to move his outside mirror. We said, "No thanks. All we need is an inch."

Phyllis hopped out with a walkie-talkie to guide Lamont in.

The man on the other side joined Phyllis. He was concerned that we would hit his RV. "It's okay. We only need an inch," Phyllis said.

In just a few minutes, with an inch to spare on either side, we were sandwiched safely between the two RVs much like the bacon and mozzarella are stuffed between two pieces of bread in this recipe.

Bacon and Mozzarella Stuffed French Toast

(Serves 2)

½	½	loaf unsliced Italian or French bread
4	4	slices cooked bacon, cut in half
1 ½ ounces	43 g	low-fat mozzarella cheese, thinly sliced
2	2	large eggs
½ cup	120 ml	orange juice
1 tablespoon	15 ml	finely chopped grated orange zest
2 tablespoons	30 ml	margarine
		maple syrup

Mark ½-inch and 1-inch measurements on the loaf of bread. At the ½–inch mark slice the bread not quite all the way through. At the 1-inch mark slice the bread all the way through. This creates pockets in the middle of the 1-inch-thick slices of bread. Do this twice.

Stuff each pocket with a layer of half the bacon and half the mozzarella cheese. Press the bread firmly together. Make sure that the bacon and cheese are tucked inside.

Whisk the eggs, orange juice, and orange zest in a bowl.

Melt the margarine in a nonstick frying pan over medium heat.

While the margarine melts, place the stuffed bread slices in the egg mixture and thoroughly coat the bread on both sides.

Fry the bread slices on each side until they are golden brown and no longer moist.

Serve the stuffed French toast with maple syrup.

Following the Mission Trail

In San Antonio, Texas, the Mission Trail gave us a glimpse at mission life in the 1700s along the San Antonio River. There are five missions. The communities were originally built of wood or adobe and later fortified with stone. Peaceful Coahuiltecan Indians living close to the missions moved into the structured compounds. In return for protection from attacking tribes, they accepted Christianity from the Spanish Franciscan priests. However, the priests gave them more than religion. Having no antibodies to protect themselves from the white man's diseases, many of the Indians died from smallpox.

Missions Conception, San Juan, San Jose, and Espada are all within an easy drive of one another. We strolled the grounds photographing adobe huts, faded frescoes, crumbled stone walls, church bells, and a moss-covered aqueduct that once carried water to the inhabitants and their crops.

The fifth mission, Alamo, sits in the middle of downtown San Antonio. In 1836, the fort that was established beside the mission became the site of the thirteen-day siege for Texas' independence from Mexico. It was in front of the mission church that Colonel William B. Travis drew his famous line in the dirt and asked any man to cross it if he was willing to fight against Mexico's General Santa Anna. Every man, except one, crossed the line. The Mexicans won the battle. All 189 men, including Davy Crockett and Jim Bowie, died in the battle.

Mexican food, like the quesadillas in this recipe, plays a major role in the cuisine of south Texas.

Breakfast Quesadillas

(Serves 2)

½	½	onion, diced
½ cup	120 ml	diced ham
1 teaspoon	5 ml	canola oil
4	4	eggs, beaten
½ cup	120 ml	diced tomato
½ cup	120 ml	salsa or chile sauce
2	2	large flour tortillas
¾ cup	180 ml	shredded cheddar cheese
¼ teaspoon	1.25 ml	salt
¼ teaspoon	1.25 ml	pepper

In a frying pan, sauté the onion and ham in the canola oil over medium heat until the onion is tender.

Add the beaten eggs, diced tomato, and salsa.

Stir to combine the ingredients until all the liquid has evaporated.

Warm the tortillas in an ungreased, heated frying pan. Place them flat and turn them until they are soft and hot.

Cover one half of each tortilla with half of the cheese. Place the egg mixture on top of the cheese. Fold the bare half of the tortilla over the egg and cheese. Cut in half and serve.

Interesting Out-of-the-Way Places

Juliette is a sleepy little town that sits at a cross-
roads in rural Georgia, just east of Forsyth and
eight miles off Interstate 75. The producers of the
movie *Fried Green Tomatoes* discovered the nearly
abandoned town. The Whistle Stop Café, made
famous by the movie, sits next to the railway tracks.
Prior to the movie, the café building was a rundown,
vacant general store and train depot. In the early days,
Juliette was a mill town that produced corn meal and
grits, the two staples of a good southern breakfast.

The Jarrell Plantation, five miles south of the
Whistle Stop Café, is now an historical site. It was a
self-sustaining farm that provided all the basic neces-
sities of life for the Jarrell family for over a century. John Jarrell invested his
money in a syrup furnace, cotton gin, steam engine, and sawmill rather than
fancy furniture and grandiose buildings. His self-sufficiency enabled the Jarrell
Plantation to rebound after the destruction caused by the Civil War.

The Jarrells settled their land in the 1840s. The descendants moved away in
1974. In the spring of 2000, we drove from pavement to gravel to dirt, to reach
the plantation. The only inhabitants, a mule and a sheep, shared a barnyard.
Where the mule went, the sheep followed. When the mule stood still, the sheep
snuggled in under its belly like a bosom buddy. An unlikely combination.

Cream cheese in French toast may seem unlikely as well, but we think it's
delicious.

Cream Cheese French Toast

(Serves 2)

4	4	fresh strawberries
6	6	slices French bread
6 tablespoons	90 ml	cream cheese
3	3	eggs
¼ cup	60 ml	skim milk
¼ teaspoon	1.25 ml	salt
¼ teaspoon	1.25 ml	pepper
		nonstick cooking oil spray
		maple syrup

Wash, trim, and slice the strawberries and set aside.

Slice the bread into ¼- to ½-inch-thick slices.

Cut each slice of bread in half.

Spread cream cheese on each piece of bread.

Put the cheese sides of the bread slices together to form cream cheese sandwich halves.

Break the eggs into a bowl and whisk them together. Add the milk, salt, and pepper. Whisk again.

Spray a frying pan with nonstick cooking oil and heat to medium-high.

Dip each half sandwich into the egg mixture and then place it in the frying pan. Fry until golden brown on both sides.

Place the French toast on a serving dish and garnish with the sliced strawberries. Serve with syrup.

A Town with Attitude

In the mid 1800s, Guerrero, Mexico, was one of the largest and most prosperous towns on the Rio Grande River. In the early 1950s, as a result of the construction of the Falcon Dam by the Mexican and American governments, Guerrero went under water after a new town with the same name was established miles away. The streets, houses, and other buildings of Old Guerrero sat beneath Falcon Lake for more than fifty years. The drought of recent times has brought back the Spanish colonial ghost town of Old Guerrero, or Guerrero Viejo.

Our tour bus lurched and bounced over ruts on the nine-mile stretch of dusty trail into the deserted town that once housed eight thousand people. Today, empty stone buildings without roofs or doors face onto rutted cobbled streets reminding us of the remains of the ancient city of Pompeii, Italy. The wind blows through the old church that still stands at the foot of the large town square. As a reminder of Old Guerrero's many years under water, seashells crunched under our feet in the dry, desert landscape. Relics of boats nestled in between the mesquite trees, cactus, and stone rubble.

Guerrero Viejo is persistent. It is a ghost town with attitude. When we visited there, one family and a herd of goats had returned to live in the town that refuses to die. These Mexican-inspired scrambled eggs have some attitude, too.

Migas
(Scrambled Eggs with Attitude)
(Serves 2)

2	2	taco shells
2	2	eggs
¼ teaspoon	1.25 ml	garlic salt
1 teaspoon	5 ml	canola oil
¼ cup	60 ml	diced onion
¼ cup	60 ml	diced tomatoes
¼ cup	60 ml	cooked, chopped bacon
¼ cup	60 ml	shredded cheddar cheese
1 tablespoon	15 ml	chopped cilantro

Cut the taco shells into small bite-sized pieces and set aside. Place the eggs and garlic salt in a bowl and whip them with a fork.

Heat the oil in a frying pan to medium-high. Add the onion, tomatoes, and bacon. Stir until the onion is translucent.

Whip the eggs one more time with a fork and add them to the frying pan. Stir constantly to mix the ingredients and cook the eggs.

When most of the moisture is gone from the eggs, add the cheese, cilantro, and taco shell pieces.

Stir until the cheese melts.

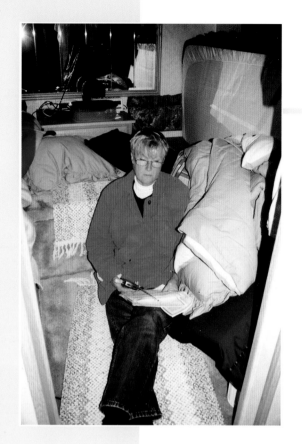

Save Time with This Tornado-Tossed Pasta

We left high winds in North Carolina, bypassed a killer tornado and torrential rains in northern Ohio, and drove into Indiana under blue skies and bright sunshine. We backed into our campsite and wondered what we should cook for dinner.

Suddenly, the alarm on our weather radio screeched. A severe thunderstorm with hailstones the size of golf balls was going to reach us within the hour. We turned on the weather channel on the television, packed the emergency suitcase, and spread out a map to track the storm. The weather radio screeched again. A tornado had been sighted just six miles away, with its anticipated path in our direction.

Normally, the first thing we do upon arriving at a new site is to locate the best and closest block or brick building for safety, in case of severe weather. At this particular site there were no such buildings. We were left to fend for ourselves in the motorhome. The best spot, we decided, was in the bedroom in the rear of the coach above the diesel motor. We created a cocoon by piling the mattresses, pillows, and spare blankets around us. We sat on the floor with the weather radio, a flashlight, and the map. Marble-sized hailstones pounded on the skylight in the bathroom. A thousand lightning bolts zigzagged across the sky. Thunder rumbled like a starving giant's stomach, but the tornado didn't touch down. The storm was over as quickly as it came.

After this disruption, we were in desperate need of food that warms and comforts. This delicious pasta was tossed together in minutes.

Chunky Pork Pasta

(Serves 4 or 5)

		nonstick cooking spray
1 ½ pounds	680 g	garlic sausage
2 tablespoons	30 ml	olive oil
4 to 6	4 to 6	whole cloves garlic, peeled
2 cups	480 ml	meatless pasta sauce
2 tablespoons	30 ml	maple syrup
1 teaspoon	5 ml	chopped fresh dill
3 cups	720 ml	cooked fusilli pasta

Spray a deep frying pan with nonstick cooking spray. Heat the frying pan to medium-high and brown the sausage.

While it is browning, prick the sausage casing in several places to prevent bursting and to release fat.

When the sausage is browned on both sides, remove it from the frying pan to cool. Rinse the frying pan.

Cut the sausage into 1-inch pieces.

In a bowl, combine the olive oil, garlic, pasta sauce, and maple syrup.

Place the pasta sauce mixture in the deep frying pan and heat to medium. Add the sausage to the pasta sauce. Cover the pan and cook for 20 minutes. Stir occasionally.

Just before serving, stir the dill into the sauce. Decrease the heat to low and cook for 2 minutes.

Serve the sausage sauce over the hot cooked pasta.

The Texas Knights Remember Their Damsels

Anyone who has traveled Interstate 10 across the bottom of Louisiana knows that it is not the smoothest road in the United States. Three years ago, somewhere between Florida and Texas, something punctured a hole in the transmission pan on our car as we towed it behind the motorhome. We did not know this until we stopped for the night at Bay Side RV Park in Palacios, Texas, on Matagorda Bay near Corpus Christi. The RV Park is nestled between rows and rows of shrimp boats. The Port of Palacios produces more shrimp than any other port in Texas.

We unhitched the vehicles and when Phyllis went to move the car so Lamont could back the motorhome into a site, the car had no transmission. Exciting as it was to be parked on the Gulf of Mexico with the expectation of a fresh catch of shrimp, we were determined to complete our trip to the Rio Grande Valley in Deep South Texas. First thing the next morning, we put on our best damsels-in-distress faces and found four knights in shining armor drinking coffee in the clubhouse. Coming to our rescue, they pushed the car into position behind the motorhome so we could hitch up. A car without a transmission was not going to stop us from reaching our destination. We towed it 300 miles (483 kilometers) south.

Recently, we stopped at the Bay Side RV Park once again. While we were there, the shrimp boats came in. We bought shrimp for this recipe. The best part of the stop was that the men in the clubhouse remembered us.

Garlic-Shrimp Pasta

(Serves 3 or 4)

3 tablespoons	45 ml	olive oil
8	8	cloves garlic, peeled, cut in half
1	1	large onion, finely chopped
1 cup	240 ml	broccoli florets
¼ cup	60 ml	finely chopped parsley
2 tablespoons	30 ml	pickled capers
1 cup	240 ml	canned chicken broth
4 cups	960 ml	cooked fusilli pasta
20	20	medium to large cooked shrimp
½ cup	120 ml	cooked and crumbled bacon fresh sprigs of parsley

Place a large, deep frying pan over medium-high heat. Add the olive oil, garlic, and onion. Stir until the onion is translucent and the garlic is tender.

Add the broccoli, parsley, capers, and chicken broth. Stir to combine the ingredients and cook until the broccoli is a bright green and not overcooked.

Add the cooked pasta and stir over the heat for 2 to 3 minutes to heat the pasta.

Toss in the cooked shrimp and crumbled bacon. Stir over the heat for 1 minute.

Place the pasta in serving dishes and garnish with sprigs of fresh parsley.

Braeburn Lodge Portions Are Big

The Braeburn Lodge, at Mile 55 on the Klondike Highway, is a popular stop for anyone traveling north in the Yukon from Whitehorse toward Dawson City. Large black-and-white magpies with blue tails squawked at the window of the log building as we chatted inside with Steve Watson, the owner. His dog was perched on top of the doghouse, eyeing the magpies. Several little pigs rooted around the doghouse.

Steve is a biker with a gray beard and a bald head. He makes and sells homemade cinnamon buns that measure close to twelve inches across. With their thick white icing and hidden pockets of cinnamon, they spill over the edges of a nine-inch dinner plate. At six dollars apiece, Steve serves between one and two hundred buns a day during the summer. Tour busses line up at his front door. A passenger from one of the tour busses took us aside and said, "I have a complaint. The guidebook says the cinnamon bun feeds four. It should say six."

"Food portions here have always been on the large size," Steve said.

Hamburgers, sandwiches, and cookies at the Braeburn Lodge are the same size as the cinnamon buns. The ten-dollar hamburger feeds two or four, depending on who is eating.

Braeburn Lodge is a checkpoint on the Yukon Dog Race as well as a stop on the Trans Canada Trail. The small airstrip across the road is called the Cinnamon Bun Strip.

We pulled back onto the Klondike Highway with a cinnamon bun that we knew would feed us for two meals. To make ourselves feel less guilty for eating that cinnamon bun, we created a healthy pasta dish.

Healthy Garlic, Broccoli, and Tomato Pasta

(Serves 4)

1 package	350 g	fettuccine noodles
10 ounces	300 ml	chicken broth
½ teaspoon	2.5 ml	salt
½ teaspoon	2.5 ml	pepper
8	8	cloves garlic
4 cups	960 ml	broccoli florets
4	4	roma tomatoes, diced
		shredded low-fat
		mozzarella cheese
		(optional)

Cook the pasta according to package's directions. Pour the pasta into a sieve and rinse with water.

Put the chicken broth in a large saucepan and add the salt, pepper, and garlic cloves.

Bring the chicken broth to a boil. Boil for 2 minutes.

Add the broccoli florets. Cook the broccoli until just tender.

Add the drained pasta to the chicken broth, garlic, and broccoli. Toss the ingredients together.

Transfer the broccoli pasta to individual serving plates. Place 2 garlic cloves on each plate.

Pile a quarter of the diced roma tomatoes on top of the pasta.

Sprinkle mozzarella around the diced tomato, if desired.

Serve immediately.

The Right Mixture Is Important in a Museum and in Meatballs

The Museum at Campbell River, British Columbia, is committed to preserving the past in order to inform the future.

A small fishing boat is on display outside the museum building. The *Soyokaze,* or "Gentle Wind," was confiscated when Japanese-Canadians lost their possessions during World War II. After the war, the original owner, Mr. Matsunaga, located the boat, bought it back, and dedicated it to the Campbell River Museum. Memorial totem poles carved by the family of Sam Henderson, a First Nations traditional chief, also stand on the museum grounds.

Inside the museum, First Nations' masks and tools of carving, fishing, and food preparation are on display. We discovered bentwood boxes made with one solid piece of bent wood. A logging exhibit includes the cross section of a 1,034-year-old tree that stood 155 feet high. The fishing exhibit contains fishing nets, floats, boats, and the history of the local canneries.

Campbell River's present embraces the culture of the First Nations, the logging and fishing industries, and the multiculturalism of the people who settled in the community on the east coast of Vancouver Island. Like the museum, these meatballs are a good mix.

Mediterranean Meatball Pasta

(Serves 4)

1 pound	454 g	ground pork
2 tablespoons	30 ml	finely chopped onion
1	1	egg
3 tablespoons	45 ml	finely diced black olives
3 tablespoons	45 ml	crumbled feta cheese
½ teaspoon	2.5 ml	garlic salt
		nonstick olive oil
		cooking spray
3 cups	720 ml	water
1	1	vegetable bouillon cube
2 tablespoons	30 ml	water
2 tablespoons	30 ml	cornstarch
4 portions	4 portions	cooked pasta
½ cup	120 ml	sliced olives
½ cup	120 ml	crumbled feta cheese

Put the ground pork in a bowl. Add the chopped onion, egg, diced black olives, crumbled feta cheese, and garlic salt. Mix the ingredients together. Make about 16 meatballs, each one about 1½ inches in diameter.

Spray a large frying pan with nonstick cooking spray and place it over medium-high heat. When the pan is hot, add the meatballs and cook until browned on all sides.

Add the water and bouillon cube and stir until the cube is dissolved. Cover the frying pan. Reduce the heat to medium and simmer for 15 minutes.

Combine the water and cornstarch in a small bowl until the mixture is smooth. Trickle the cornstarch mixture into the meatballs, stirring constantly. Stir and continue to simmer until the mixture no longer thickens. If the sauce is too thick, add a little water; if it is too thin, combine a little more cornstarch with water and slowly stir it into the hot liquid.

Serve the meatballs and sauce over cooked pasta. Garnish the dish with the sliced olives and crumbled feta cheese.

Mega Pasta Makes Use of Lucky Vegetables

Not long ago, we lost a traveling companion when we crossed the border from Canada into the United States. Her name was Colleen, and she had travelled 50,000 miles (81,000 kilometers) with us in the motorhome. Together we roamed the roads from Prince Edward Island to Vancouver Island, the Yukon to Arizona, Las Vegas to the West Edmonton Mall, California to the Florida Everglades, and all parts in between.

She was a stubborn shamrock, surviving our garage sales, our neglect to water her, and our overwatering. When she grew so tall that her leaves drooped over the edges of her pot, we gave her a brush cut, cutting her stems to within an inch of their lives. In a few days, new little shoots pushed through the soil.

Colleen was our clock and our thermometer. When her leaves huddled tightly together, we knew it was either time to go to bed or time to get out our winter coats. Her delicate white flowers blossomed in the summer sunshine; their faces turned eagerly to the world outside the motorhome as though wondering where we would take her next.

The U.S. customs officer was a man of few words. "Eggplant," he said as he opened the refrigerator to check its contents. He reached beyond the eggplant to confiscate a lemon. On his way out of the motorhome, he spoke again.

"Oh, oh," he said when he saw Colleen. "That plant's not allowed across the border." We watched in shock as he dumped her into the official U.S. garbage bin conveniently located beside his booth. He handed us an empty flowerpot.

Except for the lemon, all the vegetables traveling with us survived the border crossing to produce the following recipe. They were the lucky ones. We miss Colleen.

Mega Pasta

(Serves 3 or 4)

1	1	small eggplant, peeled and cubed
4	4	cloves garlic, cut in half
¼ cup	60 ml	extra virgin olive oil
1	1	large sweet red pepper, cut into small chunks
1	1	small Spanish onion, cut into small chunks
2 cups	480 ml	broccoli florets
3	3	tomatoes, chopped
1 teaspoon	5 ml	chopped pickled jalapeño peppers (optional)
2	2	vegetable bouillon cubes
4 cups	960 ml	cooked large rigatoni

In a large frying pan, stir and cook the eggplant and garlic in the olive oil over medium-high heat for 3 minutes.

Add the red pepper, onion, broccoli, tomatoes, jalapeño peppers, and bouillon cube. Cook 5 minutes, stirring occasionally. If the mixture is dry, add a 1 or 2 tablespoons of water.

Add the cooked pasta to the vegetables in the frying pan. Stir and cook for 3 minutes. Serve.

How We Missed the Head-Smashed-In Buffalo Jump

The Plains Indians stampeded herds of buffalo over cliffs to their deaths for more than ten thousand years. The hunters butchered and processed their kill at campsites below. The Head-Smashed-In Buffalo Jump, near Fort McLeod, Alberta, is named for a young brave who stood under a ledge of the cliff to watch the buffalo as they fell. He died when he was crushed between the animals and the cliff.

We left the main highway and followed a narrow, paved road to the buffalo jump historical site. We missed the turnoff that led to the first parking lot. The type of hitch that connects our towed vehicle to our motorhome makes it impossible for us to back up for more than a few feet. Fortunately, there was a second parking lot not too far down the road. Unfortunately, it was full.

With no place to turn around, our only choice was to forgo our visit to the buffalo jump and continue straight ahead on the narrow, paved road. A small sign said it was 22 miles (35 kilometers) to the main highway. Around the first curve, the pavement turned to gravel. Even though we drove slowly and didn't create clouds of dust like the buffalo would have done as they ran full speed toward the cliff, both the motorhome and the car were completely gray when we reached the main road.

We missed the Head-Smashed-In Buffalo Jump. This recipe is meatless.

Oodles of Noodles

(Serves 4)

4 portions	4 portions	vermicelli noodles
4 ½ tablespoons	67.5 ml	extra virgin olive oil
5	5	cloves garlic, thinly sliced
1 ½ cups	360 ml	chopped Italian parsley
3 ounces	90 ml	freshly grated Romano cheese
		freshly ground black pepper

Heat a large saucepan of water to boiling. Add 1 teaspoon of olive oil to the water. Add the vermicelli noodles.

Drain the pasta when it is cooked but firm. Do not rinse the cooked pasta.

Heat a large frying pan over medium heat and add the olive oil.

Add the sliced garlic cloves to the heated oil.

Just before the garlic begins to turn golden, stir in the chopped parsley.

Quickly transfer the drained vermicelli to the olive oil, garlic, and parsley in the frying pan while the pasta is still quite moist. Mix together using a pair of forks or tongs.

Serve the pasta topped with freshly grated Romano cheese and coarsely ground pepper.

An Experience Worth Repeating

At a quick glance, Prince Edward Island is the land of potato farms, fishing boats, Anne of Green Gables, and red soil. But we discovered that there is a lot more to the island. When we went parasailing, we learned that Dale Larkin, the owner of the Inn at the Pier, also rented personal watercraft. The personal watercraft is the warm-weather, water-borne cousin of the snowmobile.

We donned life jackets and climbed aboard our individual units. We investigated islands, dipped under bridges, and traced the contours of the Stanley River shoreline. It felt as though we were floating as we skimmed over the surface of the water. We didn't fit the popular image of the personal watercraft user, that of the noisy daredevil carving high-speed circles in the water. No roaring engines or incessant circling for us, just the wind in our faces, the power of the throttle at our fingertips, and the nearby potato fields flowing down to the shoreline.

This pasta is another of life's wonderful experiences. Not to be passed up and definitely worth repeating.

Pass da Pasta

(Serves 4)

1½ cups	360 ml	canned artichokes, not marinated
10	10	sun-dried tomatoes
6	6	cloves garlic, finely chopped
1	1	medium cooking onion, finely chopped
2 tablespoons	30 ml	olive oil
3 cups	720 ml	canned diced tomatoes
1 tablespoon	15 ml	oregano
1 pinch	1 pinch	ground basil
½ teaspoon	2.5 ml	coarse black pepper
1 teaspoon	5 ml	anise seeds
1 teaspoon	5 ml	crushed red pepper flakes
1½ cups	360 ml	canned mushroom stems and pieces
½ cup	120 ml	red wine
12 ounces	340 g	egg noodles
1 cup	240 ml	feta cheese

Cut the artichoke pieces and sun-dried tomatoes into bite-sized pieces.

Heat a deep frying pan to medium-high. Cook and stir the garlic and onion in the olive oil until the onions are translucent. Add the diced tomatoes, oregano, basil, black pepper, anise, crushed red peppers, mushrooms, artichokes, and sun-dried tomatoes.

Decrease the heat to medium and mix well. Stir in the red wine. Simmer for 15 minutes.

While the sauce is simmering, cook the egg noodles and crumble the feta cheese.

Add the artichokes to the sauce. Stir well.

Drain the noodles. Place them on a serving dish and cover them with the sauce.

Spoon the crumbled feta cheese over the hot sauce.

Tex-Mex Is More Than a Type of Cuisine

One day, we decided to cross as foot passengers into Mexico on the Los Ebonos Ferry near Mission, Texas. Named for the old ebony trees that line the riverbank, the ferry is the only existing hand-pulled ferry on the U.S.-Mexican border. It holds three cars. In about five minutes, the muscle power of seven men pulling on a cable transports the flat barge across the Rio Grande River.

Back on the Texas side of the river we visited the La Lomita Chapel hidden away among the mesquite trees. The tiny "little hill" chapel was built in 1865 as an overnight way station for Oblate padres who regularly traveled on horseback along the north side of the Rio Grande River.

In the early days, the powerful Rio Grande River sometimes changed shape as it snaked through the countryside. The nationality of some of the small towns along the river alternated through history, from Mexican to American and then back to Mexican again, as the river changed course. Today, many billboards, radio stations, conversations, and menus are in both Spanish and English in the bicultural Rio Grande Valley of southern Texas. In most grocery stores, the selection of corn and flour tortillas is larger than the selection of bread.

This pasta sauce provides a sampling of Tex-Mex, using Rio Grande Valley produce. *Es muy bueno.*

Tex-Mex Pasta

(Serves 4)

2	2	large cloves garlic, finely chopped
¼ cup	60 ml	finely diced sweet onion
2 cups	480 ml	canned diced tomatoes
1	1	small avocado, peeled and cubed
1 cup	240 ml	canned niblet corn, drained
1 teaspoon	5 ml	hot sauce
¼ teaspoon	1.25 ml	salt
¼ teaspoon	1.25 ml	pepper
¼ cup	60 ml	extra virgin olive oil
½ cup	120 ml	chopped fresh cilantro
4 servings	4 servings	fettucini noodles
		grated Parmesan cheese

Mix the garlic, onion, tomatoes, avocado, corn, hot sauce, salt, pepper, olive oil, and cilantro together in a large bowl to create the pasta sauce.

Cook the fettucini noodles according to instructions. Drain them well.

Add the hot drained pasta to the cold sauce. Toss to coat the noodles.

Sprinkle with grated Parmesan cheese and serve immediately.

Steal Someone Else's Motorhome

It was Phyllis's turn to drive. On our way through Georgia, on Interstate 75, a man in a passing convertible pointed back at our towed car. We had been warned about the "bad guys" who motion that there is something wrong with your vehicle and then, when you pull over, they force themselves aboard and either steal your money or your motorhome. We weren't about to be taken in by this man's scheme to steal our home-on-wheels. If he wanted a motorhome he would have to steal someone else's. Phyllis pushed harder on the accelerator. The monitor on the dash showed that our towed car was following along nicely. Our motorhome wasn't having any difficulty pulling it.

A second car passed us. The passenger's arms flailed out the window and his eyes bulged as he pointed to the rear of the motorhome. The sincere look on his face convinced us that it might be a good idea to pull over. Phyllis stopped the motorhome and turned on the emergency flashers. We checked the mirrors to see that no one was lingering nearby. Traffic whizzed by, rocking the entire coach from side to side. Lamont jumped out and ran back to see what was causing all the commotion.

The rear tire, on the driver's side of our towed car, had completely separated from the rim. The sidewalls of the tire had gone on a trip of their own. We made a call from our cell phone to our emergency road service. The serviceman arrived, changed the tire, and was about to drive away when we discovered that the motorhome wouldn't start. Running the emergency flashers for an hour is not a good idea.

This recipe is fast and flavorful—perfect for the end of an eventful day.

Apple-Pineapple Drumsticks

(Serves 2 or 3)

2 tablespoons	30 ml	olive oil
6	6	large chicken drumsticks
1 teaspoon	5 ml	salad herb seasoning
1 tablespoon	15 ml	pickled ginger slices
½ teaspoon	2.5 ml	pepper
1 cup	240 ml	cubed pineapple
2 cups	480 ml	apple juice
1	1	lime, juiced
½ cup	120 ml	chopped green onions

Heat the olive oil in a large, deep frying pan over medium-high heat. Brown the chicken legs on both sides.

While the chicken is browning, sprinkle the herb seasoning over top.

When both sides of the chicken legs are lightly browned, add the pickled ginger, pepper, pineapple, apple juice, and lime juice.

Decrease the heat to medium and cook for 30 minutes, or until the chicken is tender. Turn the chicken over occasionally.

Place the chicken drumsticks on serving plates and spoon the broth over top.

Sprinkle with chopped green onions. Serve.

This Is Just as Tasty Without the Squirrel

Walter and Kathryn Smith are from Durham, North Carolina. Walter had been in the Navy during the Second World War and was now retired from running his own business. When Walter looked out the front window of his motorhome and noticed that two women had driven into the RV Resort where he was staying, his instant reaction was to step out and help us.

The road into our site was paved and wide. Backing in would have been a simple task if someone hadn't parked a boat on the street.

"When I saw how well y'all could back that motorhome, I could see y'all didn't need my help," Walter said.

However, when Walter offered to teach us how to make his father's Brunswick stew we were glad for his help.

Walter's father, Pop Smith, made Brunswick stew so often for church socials that he created a special spoon in the shape of a paddle. He attached a handle to it so he could sit away from the heat of the kettle and still stir the stew the way it was required. According to Kathryn and Walter, it is the best Brunswick stew recipe in the southern United States.

Pop Smith's recipe called for thirteen large hens. Because we didn't need a recipe that would feed an entire church congregation, we have reduced the ingredients and adjusted the method. Brunswick stew was originally created to use the end-of-the-harvest vegetables from the garden. Early versions of this recipe also called for squirrel and rabbit. Substituting these for the chicken and pork is optional.

Pop Smith's Brunswick Stew

(Serves 8 to 10)

1	1	large chicken
1 pound	454 g	fresh pork leg meat
		water
5	5	large white potatoes
3	3	medium onions
56 ounces	1.68 L	canned diced tomatoes with liquid
28 ounces	840 ml	canned butter beans or small lima beans, drained
28 ounces	840 ml	canned creamed corn
1½ tablespoons	22.5 ml	sugar
¼ pound	113 g	butter
3 tablespoons	45 ml	apple cider vinegar
1 tablespoon	15 ml	salt
½ teaspoon	2.5 ml	black pepper
½ teaspoon	2.5 ml	cayenne pepper
4 tablespoons	60 ml	Worcestershire sauce

Place the chicken and pork meat in a huge pot and cover with water. Bring to a boil over high heat. Turn the heat down to bring the water to a slow boil and cook for 2 hours, or until the chicken is falling off the bone and the pork is tender.

Remove the meat from the broth. Chill the broth in the refrigerator until the grease rises to the top. Remove the chicken meat from the bones. Refrigerate the meat until ready to make the stew.

Boil and drain the potatoes. Mash the potatoes with a fork.

Peel and dice the onions.

Discard the fat from the top of the broth. Put 6 cups of the broth into a large pot. Heat to medium-high.

Cut the meat, against the grain, into pieces not longer than 2 inches. Stir the meat into the broth and cook until the chicken and pork are well mixed.

Stir in the tomatoes, beans, creamed corn, mashed potatoes, onion, sugar, butter, vinegar, salt, pepper, and cayenne pepper. Stir constantly until the mixture reaches a boil.

Reduce the heat to medium. Stir almost constantly to prevent sticking. Continue to cook slowly for 3 hours, or until no liquid is left, the consistency is very thick, and the meat has broken down into thin strands.

Remove the pot from the heat and stir in Worcestershire sauce. Serve.

Discovering Pelee Island Treasures

Pelee Island, Ontario, sits in Lake Erie on the same latitude as northern California. The population of 275 climbs to over 1,000 in the summer. Five hundred acres of the Pelee Island Winery vineyards thrive in the sun and the soil of the island. The location and temperate weather entice a mixed bag of birds, naturalists, farmers, hunters, winemakers, and tourists.

In the spring and again in the fall, people flock to Pelee Island, as well as Point Pelee National Park on the Ontario mainland, to celebrate the arrival and departure of migrating birds. The Pelee area is at the convergence of two major flyways. Migrating birds use the island as a resting-place on their flight across Lake Erie. In the fall, the Monarch butterflies begin their migration to the mountains of Mexico for the winter.

At Lighthouse Point, the now vacant Pelee Island Light is a landmark. It was the second oldest Canadian lighthouse in Lake Erie, built to help ships through the hazardous Pelee Passage.

At the ruins of Vin Villa, where the McCormick family made wine years ago, tall grass and tree branches played with the sun and shadows on the old stone walls. Half way around the path that circled the property we reached the water's edge overlooking Huldah's Rock, named for an Indian maiden. A legend tells how Huldah plunged to her death in sorrow when her English husband sailed away and never returned.

Throughout our day on the island, as we ventured from one fascinating place to another, we shared an overwhelming sensation. We felt like guests playing a game on a private island. The rules were that we had to set out on our own to discover the island's scattered treasures. We cooked this chicken using Pelee Island red wine.

Chicken in Wine

(Serves 4)

4	4	chicken drumsticks
4	4	chicken thighs
2 tablespoons	30 ml	olive oil
½	½	large onion, chopped
2	2	cloves garlic, chopped
½ teaspoon	2.5 ml	thyme
½ teaspoon	2.5 ml	pepper
½ teaspoon	2.5 ml	salt
½	½	red pepper, cut into strips
1 tablespoon	15 ml	red wine vinegar
1 cup	240 ml	dry red wine

Remove the skin and any visible fat from the drumsticks and thighs.

In a large frying pan, sauté the chicken pieces in the olive oil until the chicken is lightly browned on all sides.

Remove the chicken from the pan and set aside.

Add the onion, garlic, thyme, pepper, and salt to the pan of oil and cook until the onion slices are a light golden brown. Stir occasionally.

Add the red pepper, red wine vinegar, red wine, and chicken.

Cover the pan and cook gently for 40 minutes. Stir occasionally.

Remove the chicken from the pan. Boil the sauce rapidly for 2 minutes.

Pour the sauce over the chicken. Serve.

On Top of the World

Phyllis sometimes has a fear of heights. It depends on how active her imagination is at the time. When we had the opportunity to parasail, she had to stop and think about it. What were the odds that the rope connecting Phyllis to the boat would break when she was 1,000 feet (305 meters) up in the air? How likely was it that the boat would stall, there would be no wind to hold up the parachute, and she would plunge to the water like a rock? What were the chances that there would be a buoy right below her and she would land on it? Is it really possible to take off from, and land back on, the parasail boat without getting wet?

Experienced with Phyllis's fears, Lamont volunteered to fly first. As she lifted off in the "Jolly Jumper"–style harness and clung to the parachute straps, knuckles white and toes crossed, she wondered if she had agreed too quickly to parasail.

Later, up where the only sound was the wind blowing through her hair, Phyllis waved both arms and both legs and smiled at the boat that was just a speck in the distance. She was even thrilled when the driver of the boat dipped her feet in the water on the way back in.

Sometimes it is better to eat chicken than to be one.

Chicken Liver Topping on Boiled Potatoes

(Serves 2 or 3)

3	3	medium potatoes
1 pound	454 g	chicken livers
2	2	cloves garlic, finely chopped
4 tablespoons	60 ml	diced onion
1 teaspoon	5 ml	canola oil
2 tablespoons	30 ml	cornstarch
1½ cups	360 ml	water
1 teaspoon	5 ml	salt
½ teaspoon	2.5 ml	pepper
½ cup	120 ml	sour cream
1 teaspoon	5 ml	chopped fresh parsley or chives

Wash and peel the potatoes. Cut into thirds. Place the potatoes in a pot and cover with water. Bring them to a boil over medium-high heat.

Trim the chicken livers, removing any fat. Cut the livers into 1-inch pieces.

In a frying pan, cook and stir the garlic and onion until the onion is translucent. Keep the frying pan hot and add the chicken livers. Brown the outsides of the livers, then decrease the heat a little and continue to cook until all the pink has disappeared and the flesh is firm. Stir the chicken livers gently and often.

Mix the cornstarch with ¾ cup of the water. Stir until the mixture is smooth. Slowly add the cornstarch to the chicken livers. Stir constantly.

As the gravy thickens, add the remaining ¾ cup water, salt, and pepper. Simmer for 20 minutes.

When the potatoes are tender, drain. Place on plates.

Pour the chicken livers and their gravy over the potatoes.

Top with sour cream and chives.

Kayaking Commands Coordination

Kayaking on television looks easy. The kayakers climb into their boats from the shoreline, they slide down into the manhole, extend their legs beneath the watertight deck, and propel their kayaks effortlessly into the open water using double-bladed paddles.

Someone told us to think of a kayak as the equivalent of a sports car that offers easy maneuverability and a heightened adrenaline rush. We experienced this sports car of boats for the first time on the Orange River near Fort Myers, Florida. The person who was in charge of the rentals gave us only basic instructions: "Help yourself to paddles and a life jacket. The kayaks are down at the water. Grip the paddle in the middle. Don't dip too deep into the water. Coordinate your paddling otherwise you'll zigzag down the river."

The kayaks were built for two, not the single-person television variety. All we have to say about our descent into the kayak is that it was not graceful. Once on the water, we propelled ourselves forward by pushing our paddles against the shoreline and tree roots that rose out of the mushy bottom of a narrow stream. The stream would take us to the Orange River. Once in the flow of the river, we zigzagged wherever the current took us. The promised adrenaline rush came when we realized that our return route was against both the current and the wind. It wasn't until we were within sight of the end of our journey that our paddles dipped on the same side, at the same time. We had learned how to kayak.

It didn't take us any time at all to coordinate our technique when it came to this avocado chicken dish.

Avocado Chicken

(Serves 2)

1	1	large clove garlic
1 teaspoon	5 ml	canola oil
2	2	skinless bone-in chicken breasts
10 ounces	300 ml	cream of mushroom soup
½ cup	120 ml	water
1 cup	240 ml	diced avocado
36	36	fresh cilantro leaves
½ cup	120 ml	shredded Monterey Jack cheese
¼ teaspoon	1.25 ml	coarse black pepper

Peel, smash, and chop the garlic clove and place the chopped garlic in a deep frying pan.

Add the oil to the garlic in the frying pan and heat to a medium-high. Place the chicken breasts in the pan and brown on both sides.

Combine the mushroom soup and water in a bowl. Pour the mixture over the browned chicken breasts.

Add the avocado pieces and the cilantro leaves to the frying pan mixture.

Cover and simmer for 30 minutes.

Add the cheese and pepper. Stir the mixture until the cheese is melted and blended into the sauce.

Place the chicken breasts on serving plates and cover with the mushroom-avocado sauce. Serve.

This One-Pot Chicken Dinner Is Our Comfort Food

In an open field behind the Legion Hall, the cowboy bread cook-off is held annually in Edinburg, Texas. At the tailgates of their pickup trucks, competitors light their mesquite campfires, set up their coolers, arrange their cooking pots, and mix their flour, baking powder, salt, sugar, oil, and milk. Some add their own secret ingredient hoping it will give them the winning edge over their competitors.

Deep cast-iron pots are heated on mesquite coals. Dough is flattened, rounded, and placed in the pots. Hot coals are piled on the lids. The end product is large, flat, round bread that was for many years eaten by cowboys out on the range on both sides of the U.S.-Mexican border.

The Legion Ladies' Auxiliary sells menudo soup for two dollars. We hadn't advanced to the menudo lesson in our Spanish class, but our curiosity got the better of us. We paid our money and in return got a big Styrofoam bowl of fatty broth with a few beans and plenty of large unidentifiable floating objects. The soup also came with fresh corn tortillas. Lamont rolled up a tortilla and dunked it in the hot broth. Grease clung to the tortilla like honey on a crêpe. She had to take a bite because the Legion lady was watching. Phyllis attempted to dissect one of the unidentifiable, slippery, gray objects with her spoon.

Later, when we researched the meats and merits of menudo, we learned that those unidentifiable objects were either calves' or pigs' feet, and tripe. Menudo is said to stimulate the senses, soothe the stomach and clear the head. It is usually eaten after a night out on the town and is widely proclaimed to be a hangover antidote.

Personally, our idea of comfort food is this one-pot chicken dinner.

One-Pot Chicken Dinner

(Serves 4)

3	3	large boneless, skinless chicken breasts
1 tablespoon	15 ml	olive oil
10 ounces	300 ml	cream of celery soup
½ cup	120 ml	dry white wine
10 ounces	300 ml	chicken broth
½	½	large onion, cut in wedges
6	6	brussels sprouts, cut in half
2	2	medium potatoes, peeled and cut in eighths
12	12	peeled whole baby carrots
1	1	parsnip, peeled and cut in half-inch cubes
½ teaspoon	2.5 ml	garlic powder
½ teaspoon	2.5 ml	pepper
½ teaspoon	2.5 ml	tarragon leaves
½ teaspoon	2.5 ml	ground thyme
½ teaspoon	2.5 ml	dill weed

Cut the chicken breasts into ½- to 1-inch cubes.

In a large frying pan or wok, over medium-high heat, stir and cook the chicken in the olive oil for 5 minutes.

Turn the heat down to medium-low and stir in the celery soup, white wine, chicken broth, onion, brussel sprouts, potatoes, carrots, parsnip, garlic powder, pepper, tarragon, thyme, and dill weed.

Cook, uncovered, over medium-low heat for 45 minutes to 1 hour. Stir occasionally. If the liquid runs low before the vegetables are cooked, add a little water.

Ladle into deep plates and serve with crusty bread.

Another Bright Idea

Thomas Edison had many bright ideas. The incandescent light bulb, the phonograph, the motion picture camera, and the storage battery are his better known ones. To acquire his many patents, he must have invented something weekly. We can relate to that as we compose weekly newspaper columns.

An obsession of Edison's, later in his life, was to try to make rubber tires out of goldenrod. His intention was to create a new source of rubber for his friend Henry Ford's automobiles. Despite his persistence and intense experimentation, goldenrod never did produce good rubber. We can relate to that as well. Some recipe ideas just don't come together as planned.

The Edison and Ford families spent time in their neighboring winter homes in Fort Myers, Florida. The Edison grounds in the lush subtropical climate of southwestern Florida are filled with many varieties of exotic plants. The gigantic banyan tree outside the reception area exhibits the characteristics of the East Indian fig tree. It sends shoots out of its branches to grow down to the soil and root, forming secondary trunks.

The idea for this recipe came from the numerous species of orange trees we saw on our tour of Edison's estate. The best thing about this recipe, besides the fantastic flavor, is that it is quick and easy to make. We think it is definitely one of our brighter ideas.

Orange-Spice Chicken Drumsticks

(Serves 2)

4	4	chicken drumsticks
½ teaspoon	2.5 ml	garlic powder
½ teaspoon	2.5 ml	ground coriander
½ teaspoon	2.5 ml	ground ginger
½ teaspoon	2.5 ml	curry powder
½ teaspoon	2.5 ml	anise
2 tablespoons	30 ml	olive oil
1	1	chicken bouillon cube
1 cup	240 ml	warm water
½	½	orange

Rinse the chicken drumsticks and remove the skin. Pat the drumsticks with paper towels to dry.

In a bowl, mix the garlic powder, ground coriander, ground ginger, curry powder, and anise.

Rub the spice mixture over the drumsticks until coated.

In a frying pan over medium heat, brown the chicken drumsticks in the olive oil for about 5 minutes, or until lightly browned on all sides.

Dissolve the chicken bouillon cube in the warm water. Pour this into the frying pan with the chicken.

Cut the half orange into 6 wedges. Do not peel the orange. Add the orange wedges to the frying pan.

Cover the frying pan tightly and cook the chicken over medium heat for about 30 minutes, or until the chicken is cooked through. If necessary, add a little extra water part way through the cooking to prevent the frying pan from going dry. Garnish with fresh orange slices. Serve.

Leave It to the Beaver

We ventured off the Cassiar Highway, in northern British Columbia, to see the totem poles in the remote First Nations village of Gitanyow. The road took us through green hills with mountains in the distance. Purple fireweed blossoms spread between the road and the swift stream that ran south to the Skeena River.

Fifteen-year-old Jaye Turley greeted us at the small museum. He had recently returned from ten days at camp in the mountains where he went to learn some of the old ways of his people. He learned how to smoke fish, shoot moose, and live off the land.

"I want to learn my culture," Jaye explained.

Jaye's granny lives in the mountains. Jay told us that she can produce seventeen cases of canned fish in the time that Jaye manages to do one or two. Jaye also told us that the blue grouse up in the mountains are as large as turkeys. And that they taste like turkey. He and the elders at the camp also caught groundhogs and beaver. Jaye said that groundhog tastes like chicken.

Jaye smiled when we asked him what beaver tastes like. "Beaver tastes like the water it lives in. We smoke it to make it taste like jerky."

As we were talking, we heard a rustle in the nearby trees. Jaye said, "It's likely a bear but it could be the spirits. There are stories that people see spirits across the river. They say the spirits are happy that the teenagers are learning their culture."

We didn't cook beaver, but from Jaye's description we can imagine what it tastes like. Perhaps it needs a simmering pot of cranberry broth to enhance the flavor.

Simmering-Pot Cranberry Chicken

(Serves 4)

1	1	whole chicken
13 ounces	390 ml	canned cranberry sauce
1½ cups	360 ml	sweet apple cider
3	3	cloves garlic, peeled and thinly sliced
½ teaspoon	2.5 ml	salt
½ teaspoon	2.5 ml	pepper
1 teaspoon	5 ml	dried basil
3	3	large potatoes
4 tablespoons	60 ml	cornstarch
½ cup	120 ml	water

Wash the chicken, peel off the skin, and remove all fat.

In a large pot, add cranberry sauce, apple cider, garlic, salt, pepper, and basil.

Stir and bring the liquid to a boil over high heat.

Decrease the heat to medium and add the chicken.

Cover the pot and simmer the chicken for 30 minutes.

Peel the potatoes and cut into quarters.

Turn the chicken over. Add the potatoes to the pot and simmer for 30 more minutes.

Remove the chicken and the potatoes to a serving platter. Cover with foil.

Remove excess fat from the cranberry broth in the pot.

Mix the cornstarch with the water until it is smooth.

Stir the cornstarch mixture into the cranberry broth. Bring the gravy to a boil over medium heat. Cook, stirring constantly, for 3 to 4 minutes. Serve with the chicken and potatoes.

The Bishop's Boiled Boots

The Old Log Church in Whitehorse, Yukon, was built in 1900 for the Church of England. The restored church is now a museum that displays artifacts of the early day missions among the Inuit and First Nations people.

A display of tattered and weathered animal-skin clothing caught our attention. The hundred-year-old remnants belonged to a certain Bishop Stringer who was otherwise known as "The Bishop Who Ate His Boots."

Bishop Stringer and a companion started out on a 500-mile (805-kilometer) trek to Dawson City. It was winter. They took limited provisions because they planned to hunt and fish along the way. From the beginning the two men struggled through icy cold water and frozen, tangled underbrush. At some point their guide deserted them. On top of that, their compass didn't work. The river they followed was frozen. The ice was so thick they couldn't fish for food. To make matters worse, they couldn't see the direction of the water flow and took a wrong turn.

The men rationed their provisions, eating just a little each day. They managed to shoot grouse and pick berries, but eventually they were down to making a soup with the last of their bacon and slim scrapings from their flour bag. For their final desperate meal, they boiled and then toasted the soles and tops of the Bishop's sealskin boots. According to the Bishop's diary, the soles tasted better than the tops. The two men survived to make it to an Indian settlement and then on to Dawson City. Both lost fifty pounds in the process.

We don't know if there were any leftover boiled boots. We recommend leftover chicken or turkey for this easy, tasty stew.

Chicken or Turkey Stew
from Leftovers

(Serves 2)

2 cups	480 ml	water
2	2	chicken bouillon cubes
2	2	potatoes, cut into cubes
1	1	onion, cut into ½-inch pieces
1	1	carrot, cut into large coins
1½ cups	360 ml	cubed cooked chicken or turkey
1 tablespoon	15 ml	cornstarch
1 tablespoon	15 ml	water
4 tablespoons	60 ml	craisins (sweetened, dried cranberries)
¼ teaspoon	1.25 ml	ground sage
¼ teaspoon	1.25 ml	dried thyme

Combine the water and bouillon cubes in a saucepan over medium-high heat. When the cubes are dissolved add the potatoes, onion, and carrot. Bring the mixture to a boil, then decrease the heat to a slow boil. Cook until the vegetables are tender.

Add the cooked chicken and continue to cook until the meat heats through.

Combine the cornstarch and water and stir until the mixture is smooth.

Slowly add the cornstarch mixture to the hot chicken stew, stirring to mix it thoroughly.

Add the craisins, sage, and thyme and continue to stir. If the stew is a little too thin, repeat the cornstarch and water mixture.

Continue to cook for 5 to 10 minutes to blend the flavors. Serve.

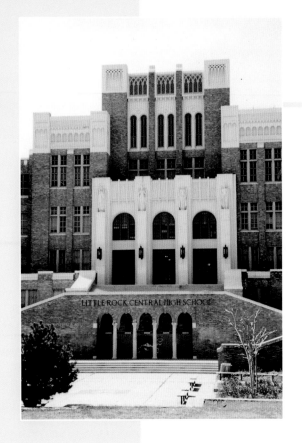

Memories of Little Rock

In the 1950s, Little Rock, Arkansas, and especially Central High School, came to symbolize the American government's commitment to eliminating separate systems of education for blacks and whites. At first, the black students were blocked from entering the school by Arkansas National Guard troops. Three weeks later, they were escorted to school and protected by U.S. federal troops ordered by President Eisenhower. Black-and-white television of the time showed the world how white adults jeered and spit at the black teenagers.

We stepped back in time at the Central High School National Historic Site. The visitor's center occupies a 1957 Mobil service station across from the school. Its restored shiny red-and-white gas pumps look just the way they did in the fifties. Inside the center, we watched old newscasts covering the events of Little Rock's desegregation period. The familiar CBS test pattern was followed by dramatic scenes of the nine black students as they struggled each day to attend the all-white Central High.

We walked the sidewalk in front of the high school. The school's façade is the same as it was in 1957. Black students and white students were studying together under a tree.

This easy thirty-minute recipe makes it possible to spend more time sightseeing.

Thirty-Minute Chicken and Rice

(Serves 2)

1 tablespoon	15 ml	canola oil
1 cup	240 ml	diced dried apricots
1 cup	240 ml	chopped onion
10 ounces	300 ml	low-salt chicken broth
1 teaspoon	5 ml	soy sauce
¼ teaspoon	1.25 ml	black pepper
2	2	boneless, skinless chicken breasts
¾ cup	180 ml	instant rice

In a large frying pan or wok, heat the oil over medium heat. Stir and cook the apricots and onions for 3 minutes.

Add the chicken broth, soy sauce, and the black pepper. Stir.

Add the chicken breasts to the pan.

Cover the pan and cook the chicken for 20 minutes, or until tender.

Add the instant rice. Stir to mix the rice with the liquid.

Cover the pan again and remove the pan from the heat. Let the rice and chicken stand covered for 5 minutes.

Stir and serve.

Christina's World Is an Inspiration

When we were in Cushing, Maine, we took a drive out to the Olsen House where Andrew Wyeth, the American painter, was inspired for his famous painting *Christina's World*.

The empty house where Christina Olsen once lived with her brother stands on a hill. Its windows overlook the sea. We met Andrew's brother-in-law, Dudley, an eighty-six-year-old raconteur. He pointed out the particular vistas and rooms of the house that inspired the artist.

Later, we joined Dudley in the garden. He asked if we could identify the vine that covered the outside wall of the house. We recognized it as hops. Dudley explained that it would appear odd for a teetotalling family to be growing hops outside the kitchen window. Apparently, in the early days, if yeast was unavailable, hops were used to make bread. A hops tea was made, and the liquid used as the leavening agent.

Dudley had to admit that the bread made from hops, with its flavor reminiscent of beer, was a nice change. In her modest world, Christina was a creative cook.

Of course the idea of substituting one thing for another in a recipe is not new. The pork rind breading in the following recipe is an interesting change from the normal bread crumbs.

Chicken Cutlet with Pork Rind Breading

(Serves 2)

2	2	boneless, skinless chicken breasts
1 ½ cups	360 ml	pork rinds
½ teaspoon	2.5 ml	garlic powder
1 tablespoon	15 ml	Parmesan cheese
1 tablespoon	15 ml	chopped fresh parsley
1	1	egg
⅛ cup	30 ml	olive oil
4	4	lemon wedges

Place chicken breasts, one at a time, under a plastic bag. The plastic bag prevents splattering. With the flat side of a meat pounder, pound the chicken breasts until thin.

Remove several pork rinds from their package and place them in a small, clear plastic bag. Crunch them by pressing on the bag. Repeat this until there are 1 ½ cups of finely crushed pork rinds. Put the crushed pork rinds in a bowl. Discard any large hard pieces of rind.

Add the garlic powder to the crushed pork rinds and combine.

In a small bowl, mix the grated Parmesan with the chopped parsley. Set aside.

In a bowl, beat the egg with a fork. Dip the chicken into the beaten egg until well coated.

Then, dip the chicken into the pork rind and garlic mixture.

Heat the oil in a large, deep frying pan over medium heat for 15 seconds.

Fry the chicken breasts in the oil for 4 minutes on each side, or until the breading is golden brown and the chicken is no longer pink in the center.

Place the cooked chicken cutlets on paper towels to remove excess oil before putting them on a serving plate.

Serve with grated Parmesan cheese and parsley mixture sprinkled on top of each cutlet. Decorate the plate with lemon wedges for squeezing. Serve.

A Quick Solution to a Chicken Problem

Chickens are protected in Key West, Florida. When we were at the Blue Heaven Restaurant, we found more chicken under the tables, on the chairs and scratching the earth around our feet than on the menu.

Apparently, after generations of living on the streets, these hens, roosters, and baby chicks are considered to be wild birds and are protected by a city ordinance that prohibits luring, seizing, or teasing. They roost in hedges at night and strut the streets during the day. Locals who are disturbed by early morning cock-a-doodle-doos throw ice cubes at the red-crowned creatures. The advantage of throwing ice cubes, instead of rocks, is that the evidence melts. Some people even go so far as to capture a particularly annoying bird, in the dark of night, and move it into someone else's neighborhood.

We have come up with a quick solution to their chicken problem.

Zesty Chicken Bites

(Serves 4)

4	4	boneless, skinless chicken breasts
2 tablespoons	30 ml	barbecue sauce
1 tablespoon	15 ml	Worcestershire sauce
2 tablespoons	30 ml	lemon juice
¼ teaspoon	1.25 ml	salt
¼ teaspoon	1.25 ml	pepper
2 to 3	2 to 3	cloves garlic, crushed
½ tablespoon	7.5 ml	dried basil leaves
½ teaspoon	2.5 ml	paprika
½ teaspoon	2.5 ml	crushed red pepper flakes
2 tablespoons	30 ml	olive oil
1 cup	240 ml	cooked rice

Trim the chicken breasts of any fat. Cut the chicken into cubes.

In a bowl, create a sauce by combining the barbecue sauce, Worcestershire sauce, lemon juice, salt, pepper, garlic, basil, paprika, and red pepper flakes.

In a frying pan, heat the olive oil and cook the chicken cubes over medium-high heat for 5 minutes, or until browned and no longer pink. Stir often.

Turn the heat down to low. Pour the sauce over the chicken.

Stir and simmer for 3 minutes.

Serve the chicken bites and sauce over the cooked rice.

This Grapefruit-Marinated Chicken Is Good, No Bull

Mercedes is the home of the South Texas Music Festival. For four days in February, musicians compete in playing the fiddle, banjo, harmonica, and guitar. There are yodeling, songwriting, and singing contests and lessons. Cloggers tap their toes and impromptu jam sessions entertain the crowds. There is a bull chip throwing contest for those who want to be a part of the festival but who can't sing, dance, or play a musical instrument.

We inspected the table of bull chips and confirmed that they were, as we suspected, what we call cow pies or cow patties. Men, women, and children all got into the competition. One man stepping up to the throw line announced that he had been shooting the bull all morning, he might as well throw it in the afternoon.

The chips are air dried and odorless and, according to the rules, have to be over six inches in diameter. The record toss is over two hundred feet (sixty-one meters). Two throws for five dollars; the money goes to scholarships at the local high school.

This chicken recipe is really good. No bull.

Grapefruit-Marinated Chicken

(Serves 3)

2 tablespoons	30 ml	olive oil
1 tablespoon	15 ml	minced garlic
¾ cup	180 ml	grapefruit juice
2 tablespoons	30 ml	soy sauce
1 tablespoon	15 ml	balsamic vinegar
2 tablespoons	30 ml	brown sugar
3	3	boneless chicken breasts
2 teaspoons	10 ml	canola oil
1 cup	240 ml	cooked rice
		red or pink grapefruit slices

Mix the olive oil, garlic, grapefruit juice, soy sauce, balsamic vinegar, and brown sugar together to make the marinade.

Place the chicken breasts in a flat glass dish and pour the marinade over them. Cover, refrigerate, and marinate for 24 hours. Turn the chicken once or twice while marinating.

Remove the chicken from the refrigerator and discard the marinade.

Cut the marinated chicken breasts into strips.

Heat the canola oil to medium-high in a non-stick frying pan. Add the chicken strips.

Turn the chicken strips until they are browned and cooked through.

Serve over cooked rice with fresh red or pink grapefruit slices as a garnish.

A Hot Pot Roast
for Sam McGee

Dawson City, Yukon, is an historic town, a real town, where everything is still in frontier mode even though camper trucks, sports utility vehicles, and motorhomes have replaced the horses and mules that transported the miners during the gold rush in the 1890s. Like their predecessors, the vehicles are piled high with supplies. Spare tires, extra gas cans, and emergency water containers are strapped to roofs and rear bumpers.

We parked at the Gold Rush Campground located right in the center of town. From there we walked the boardwalks to the Gaslight Follies at the Palace Grand Theatre, where the stage show provides a humorous glimpse at life during the gold rush days. Just down the street at Diamond Tooth Gerties Gambling Hall and Can Can Show, the girls whoop and talk as they dance, vying for the attention of the men in the audience just as the dancers did over a hundred years ago.

Robert Service's restored log cabin sits on a hill above the town. Sod grows on the roof. A young man portrays the Bard of the Yukon twice a day during the summer months. He reminisces about life in the north and reads from the poet's works. We learned that Sam McGee, the title character in *The Cremation of Sam McGee*, was a real person from Peterborough, Ontario. When Service's poem became famous, McGee's life changed forever. No matter where he was from that point on, people approached him and asked, "Is it warm enough for you, Sam?"

This pot roast recipe would fortify any gold miner who was about to embark on the quest for gold.

Eye-of-the-Round Pot Roast

(Serves 4)

3 cups	720 ml	water
4 tablespoons	60 ml	tomato paste
1	1	beef bouillon cube
1 teaspoon	5 ml	garlic salt
3 teaspoons	15 ml	dried minced onion
2 pounds	907 g	eye-of-the-round beef roast
2	2	potatoes, cubed (optional)
2	2	carrots, cubed (optional)
1	1	onion, cubed (optional)
1 cup	240 ml	turnip, cubed (optional)
1	1	parsnip, cubed (optional)
1	1	stalk celery, cubed (optional)

Combine the water, tomato paste, beef bouillon cube, garlic salt, and dried onion in a heavy pot that is large enough that the roast will not touch the sides. Heat the mixture and stir until the bouillon cube is dissolved.

Place the roast in the pot and cover tightly.

Cook on a medium-low heat for 2 ½ hours, or until the meat is tender.

Turn the roast every 30 minutes to prevent it from sticking.

Add the vegetables during the last 30 minutes of cooking.

When the pot roast is tender, remove it from the broth to a cutting board. Allow the meat to cool for 10 to 15 minutes. Slice the meat and set aside.

The vegetables can continue to cook in the broth while the meat cools. If the broth is too thick, add a little water.

Remove the vegetables to a serving dish. Return the sliced beef to the hot broth for 3 or 4 minutes to reheat, if necessary. Place the meat on a serving platter. Pour the broth into a gravy boat and serve.

Barkerville Is Still a Boomtown

The Fraser Bridge Inn and RV Park in downtown Quesnel, British Columbia, was an ideal spot for us to stop for a night as we traveled north along the Fraser River through the province of British Columbia. From Quesnel we followed the Gold Rush Trail to historic boomtown Barkerville. The former four-hour stagecoach trip took us twenty-five minutes. Between 1862 and 1870, over one hundred thousand people traveled this Cariboo Wagon Road in search of gold.

Barkerville, British Columbia, is a town that is so authentically late-1800s that the conversations of twenty-first century actors and adventuresome tourists, dressed in the clothing of the 1870s, revolve around the gold rush and the gossip of the day. Rain barrels sit precariously on the rooftops of heritage buildings, in the event of fire. A stagecoach works its way among the visitors on the main street. The post office provides full postal services. A schoolmistress rings the schoolbell and questions nearby children about their homework. The Cariboo Sentinel Print Shop produces a daily newspaper. Cheese, cold cuts, and teas are available in the Drygoods Store. The Lung Duck Tong Restaurant, named after a fraternal organization of the Chinese immigrants who came to British Columbia in search of gold, offers dim sum, the small seafood, meat, mushroom, and chestnut delicacies that were available to the Chinese men in the days of the gold rush.

There are no hamburgers in Barkerville, past or present. If we had been around in the 1870s, we could have whipped up this hardy hamburger hash for the exhausted miners. We might even have traded it for a gold nugget or two.

Hamburger Hash

(Serves 2 or 3)

		nonstick cooking spray
½ pound	*227 g*	*lean ground beef*
1	*1*	*onion, chopped*
3 tablespoons	*45 ml*	*cornstarch*
1½ cups	*360 ml*	*water*
14 ounces	*397 g*	*tomato sauce*
2	*2*	*carrots, sliced into thin circles*
1	*1*	*large celery stalk, finely chopped*
1 cup	*240 ml*	*chopped cabbage*
½ teaspoon	*2.5 ml*	*salt*
½ teaspoon	*2.5 ml*	*pepper*
½ teaspoon	*2.5 ml*	*thyme*
½ teaspoon	*2.5 ml*	*basil*
1 cup	*240 ml*	*cooked rice or macaroni*

Heat a large frying pan to medium-high and spray it with the nonstick oil. Brown the ground beef. When the meat is dry and the pan is browning, add the onions. Cook until the onions are translucent. Remove the pan from the heat.

Combine the cornstarch and water in a small bowl and pour it into the frying pan. Mix well.

Return the pan to medium heat and add the tomato sauce, carrots, celery, and cabbage. Simmer for 30 minutes, stirring occasionally.

While the ingredients are simmering add the salt, pepper, thyme, and basil. Add a trickle of water if the hash becomes too thick.

When the vegetables are tender, stir in the rice or macaroni. Heat through and serve.

Serve a Crowd with This Amish Haystack Dinner

In Goshen, Indiana, the parents' group of a local Amish school served a meal to two thousand RV owners. All day the cooks sliced, chopped, browned, and stirred under a tent in the hot sun. We arrived at mealtime, picked up our beverage, and took a seat at a long table that was set with a piece of home-made pie at every place. Within minutes we were welcomed to the buffet table where we selected a dinner plate and passed it to the first of a long line of servers. As we walked the length of the table our plate was passed from server to server. Each server dished up a different food item until our meal was piled like a haystack. First soda crackers, then rice, lettuce, tortilla chips, tomatoes, green peppers, onion, meat sauce, and finally, cheese sauce. When the plate was returned to us, it had to be held with both hands.

Much like an exaggerated taco salad, the haystack was tasty, very filling, and definitely entertaining. The pie was good, too. We know it's not a normal thing to cook for two thousand people, so we've adjusted the quantities to serve three or four.

Haystack Dinner

(Serves 3 or 4)

1½ cups	360 ml	crumbled soda crackers
3 cups	720 ml	cooked rice
¼	¼	head lettuce, shredded
1½ cups	360 ml	crumbled tortilla chips
1½ cups	360 ml	diced tomatoes
½	½	green pepper, finely diced
¼	¼	large onion, finely diced
1 pound	454 g	extra lean ground beef
1 cup	240 ml	pizza sauce
3 ounces	90 ml	water
2 teaspoons	10 ml	chili powder
¼ teaspoon	1.25 ml	cumin
¼ teaspoon	1.25 ml	cayenne pepper
4 tablespoons	60 ml	butter
4 tablespoons	60 ml	flour
½ teaspoon	2.5 ml	salt
2 cups	480 ml	skim milk
2 cups	480 ml	grated cheddar cheese

Prepare the soda crackers, rice, lettuce, tortilla chips, tomatoes, green pepper, and onion and set them aside. The rice can be reheated later.

To make the meat sauce, brown the ground beef in a frying pan. Drain off any excess grease.

Add the pizza sauce and water to the cooked meat. Stir well.

Add the chili powder, cumin, and cayenne pepper to the meat and simmer for 10 minutes. Set aside.

For the cheese sauce, melt the butter in a saucepan over low heat. Remove from the heat. Stir in the flour until the mixture is smooth.

Add the salt and milk and mix well. Cook over low heat, stirring constantly, until the sauce thickens.

Add the cheese and continue to stir until smooth and creamy. Do not leave cheese sauce unattended over the heat or it will burn.

Reheat the rice and the meat sauce. When the cheese sauce is complete, the dish is ready to put together.

On each plate, create a stack by piling one ingredient on top of the other. Layer the ingredients starting with the crumbled soda crackers on the bottom, then the cooked rice, shredded lettuce, crumbled tortilla chips, diced tomatoes, diced green pepper, diced onion, and the meat sauce.

Top each stack with a generous layer of cheese sauce and serve.

Bridging the Gap Between Ordinary and Outstanding

We were very aware of the river gushing over the rocks 70 meters (230 feet) below us as we ventured onto the Capilano Suspension Bridge in West Vancouver, British Columbia. We gripped the heavy cord railing tightly as we walked the 137 meters (449 feet) across the gorge. Douglas Fir, Sitka Spruce, Western Red Cedar, and Western Hemlock (the four main types of trees in British Columbia) can be found in the dense forest along the Capilano River. The Douglas Fir, the largest cone-bearing tree in the province, reaches an average height of 61 meters (200 feet) and can live to be 1,200 years old.

Crossing over the river on a swinging bridge can be a challenge for anyone with a fear of heights. The view was outstanding.

The combination of flavors in the following recipe bridges the gap between ordinary and outstanding liver.

Liver and Canadian Back Bacon

(Serves 3 or 4)

4 tablespoons	60 ml	olive oil

1	1	medium onion, cut into rings
4 to 6	4 to 6	slices cured Canadian back bacon (pork backs)
1¼ pounds	568 g	fresh beef liver, sliced all-purpose flour
3 cups	720 ml	canned diced tomatoes, undrained
1	1	beef bouillon cube
¼ teaspoon	1.25 ml	pepper
½ cup	120 ml	red wine
½ cup	120 ml	chopped fresh parsley

Heat 2 tablespoons of the olive oil over medium heat in a large nonstick frying pan for about 1 minute.

Add the onion rings and stir fry until the onions are a light golden color. Remove the onion rings from the pan and set them on a plate.

Cut each piece of back bacon in half. Add the back bacon to the pan and fry until the bacon is light golden brown on each side. Remove the pan from the heat and remove the bacon from the pan to a plate.

Dry the liver with a paper towel and cut the slices into manageable pieces.

Sprinkle some flour on a plate and coat the liver lightly with the flour.

Return the pan to medium heat and add the remaining 2 tablespoons olive oil.

Add the liver to the pan and fry until the liver is lightly browned on both sides. Add a little extra olive oil if needed.

Place the onion rings and the bacon on top of the liver. Spread the canned tomatoes over the onion, bacon, and liver.

In a small bowl, mix the beef bouillon cube and the pepper into the red wine until the bouillon cube is broken into small pieces.

Pour the wine mixture over the tomatoes in the frying pan.

Bring the pan ingredients to a boil, stir gently, and reduce the heat to low. Cover the pan and cook for 15 minutes.

Remove the lid from the pan and cook for 30 more minutes. Stir occasionally so the liver doesn't stick.

Remove the pan from the heat and place the food on a serving dish. Sprinkle chopped fresh parsley over the top and serve.

Watch This New Mexico Chile Disappear

Gila Cliff Dwellings National Monument is north of Silver City in southwestern New Mexico. It offers a glimpse of the homes and lives of the people of the Mogollon culture who lived in the Gila Wilderness from the 1280s through the early 1300s and then mysteriously disappeared. In five of the seven cavities in the face of the cliff there are forty-two rooms. The topography surrounding the caves probably looks today very much like it did when the cliff dwellings were inhabited. The magnificent hills and valleys must have been difficult to leave.

We discovered that, although the distance on State Highway 15 north from Silver City to the Gila Cliff Dwellings is only 43 miles (69 kilometers), it took about two hours to get there by car. Anyone driving a vehicle over 20 feet (6 meters) in length would face a challenge on the twisting and turning mountain road. We were glad we didn't take our motorhome.

In New Mexico, a bowl of chile, spelled with an *e*, does not get its spicy taste from chili powder. It is made with red hot chile pepper pods. The seeds and membranes of the dried peppers are removed so there is no heat, just the natural chile pepper flavor. Our New Mexico chile begins with the local staples of onions, chiles, and pinto beans. New Mexico chile always contains potatoes.

A bowl of this chile will disappear just like the Gila Cliff Dwellers.

New Mexico Chile

(Serves 4 or 5)

3 ounces	85 g	dried, large, red hot chile pepper pods
8 cups	1.9 L	boiling water
4 tablespoons	60 ml	diced onion
3	3	large cloves garlic, chopped
2 tablespoons	30 ml	canola oil
1	1	beef bouillon cube
2 tablespoons	30 ml	white sugar
1 teaspoon	5 ml	cumin
¼ teaspoon	1.25 ml	salt
2 tablespoons	30 ml	cornstarch
3 tablespoons	45 ml	water
1 pound	454 g	extra lean ground beef
1	1	large onion, diced
4 cups	960 ml	canned pinto beans, drained and rinsed
2	2	cooked potatoes, peeled and cut into ½-inch cubes

Cut the stems off the dried chile peppers. Cut a slit down one side of each pod and remove the seeds and their adjoining membrane.

Cover the peppers with the boiling water and soak for 20 minutes.

Put peppers and ¼ cup of the soaking liquid into a blender and purée. Save the remaining liquid. Press the purée through a strainer to remove any remaining seeds and skin.

Cook the onion and garlic in the canola oil until the onions are translucent. Add the purée to the onion and garlic. Add 3 cups of the soaking liquid to the purée mixture.

Break up the bouillon cube. Add it and the sugar, cumin, and salt to the purée mixture. Bring it to a boil, then decrease the heat to a simmer. Simmer for 5 minutes.

In a small bowl, combine the cornstarch and water into a paste. Stir continuously while adding the paste to the red chile sauce. Simmer for 10 minutes, stirring occasionally. Remove the red chile sauce from the heat and set it aside.

Stir and brown the ground beef in a large, deep frying pan, cooking it thoroughly.

Add the diced onion and cook until it is translucent.

Add the pinto beans, potatoes, and red chile sauce. Mix well. Cook for 15 minutes. Ladle into bowls and serve.

Oktoberfest Is Barrels of Fun

The biggest Bavarian festival in North America happens in Kitchener-Waterloo, Ontario. Every year in early October, the twin cities uncork the beer barrel to signify the beginning of Oktoberfest. We look forward to sampling the German food, kicking up our heels to the Beer Barrel Polka, doing the chicken dance, and sitting on the sidelines for the largest Thanksgiving Day parade in Canada.

Oktoberfest in Munich, Germany, is the largest celebration of its kind in the world. Oktoberfest began in the early 1800s when King Ludwig married Princess Therese von Sachesen-Hildenburghausen. Horse races were held to celebrate the happy occasion. The horse races became an annual event and were combined with the state agricultural fair. By the late 1800s, the event included large beer and food tents.

In the true spirit of Gemütlichkeit, we want to share this German recipe. We spent many hours each week in our restaurant preparing these beef bundles. They go well with pickled red cabbage, boiled potatoes, and, in the true German tradition, a glass of cold beer. It is Wunderbar.

These rouladen can be made ahead and reheated. Add a little water to thin the gravy when reheating.

Rouladen

(Serves 8)

3 tablespoons	45 ml	canola oil
2	2	large cooking onions, sliced into rings ⅛ to ¼ inch thick
16	16	strips lean bacon
8	8	thinly sliced inside round steaks (less than ⅛ inch thick and about 9 inches long, 5 inches wide)
		salt
		pepper
¼ cup	60 ml	prepared mustard
16	16	dill pickle slices, thinly sliced lengthwise
½ cup	120 ml	flour
4 cups	960 ml	water
1	1	chicken bouillon cube
½ teaspoon	2.5 ml	garlic salt
¼ teaspoon	1.25 ml	black pepper

Place 1 tablespoon of the oil in a frying pan over medium-low heat. Cook the onion rings until they are limp and tender but not browned. Set aside. Fry the bacon until it is partially cooked. Drain on paper towels. Set aside.

Place the steaks flat on the kitchen counter with the widest end at the front. Sprinkle the meat lightly with salt and pepper. Spread ½ tablespoon of prepared mustard evenly on each slice. Divide the onion rings into 8 bundles and place a bundle at the widest end of each piece of meat. Place 2 pickle slices and 2 slices of bacon on top of each bundle of onion rings.

Roll up the steak, cabbage-roll-style, tucking in the ends. Secure the loose ends with toothpicks. Push the toothpicks in and out, as though sewing, so they lie flat for easy frying. Put the 2 remaining tablespoons of oil in a large frying pan and heat to medium-high. When the oil is hot, brown the rouladen on all sides. Remove the meat to a platter. Cover the frying pan with a splatter guard and cook to reduce the remaining liquid until it is thick and golden brown.

Turn off the heat and add the flour to the liquid. If the pan is dry, add 1 tablespoon of oil. Scrape any brown coloring from the sides of the pan into the flour. Mix the flour and oil thoroughly then add the water a little at a time and whisk until smooth. Heat the liquid to medium-high and stir. When the gravy is thick and smooth, add the chicken bouillon cube, garlic salt, and black pepper. If there are lumps pour the gravy through a sieve and then return it to the pan.

Gently remove the toothpicks from the rouladen and place the meat in the gravy. Cook with a slow boil for 1½ hours, or until the meat is very tender. Occasionally turn the rouladen in the gravy. Serve.

A Work of Art

We attended the annual Waterloo County and Area Quilt Festival. In fact, we spent an entire week admiring and touching quilts. We learned that whether it serves as a comforter on a bed or as an art piece on a wall, a quilt tells a story through its symbols, colors, stitches, and textures. A finished quilt is a signature of the artist or artists who created it. It is a work of art.

Each spring, along with the Quilt Festival, the Ontario Mennonite Relief Sale is held in nearby New Hamburg, Ontario. It is one of Canada's largest quilt auctions. The arena comes alive with the sound of the auctioneer as the crowd strains to see who is bidding on each new quilt that appears on the stage.

With the artistry of the quilt festival around us, and without a sewing skill between us, we decided to stick to what we know best. We are also not convinced that we have the patience it takes to make a quilt. Most of our food creations take much less time to create. If flavors could be described as works of art, this dish would be our signature quilt. It takes time and patience to prepare, but the finished product is worth all the effort.

Melt-in-Your-Mouth Sauerbraten

(Serves 8 to 10)

2 pounds	908 g	eye-of-the-round roast
		prepared mustard
		salt
		pepper
2	2	onions, diced
2 cups	480 ml	white vinegar
2 cups	480 ml	water
2	2	whole cloves
4	4	bay leaves
12	12	peppercorns
2 tablespoons	30 ml	white sugar
2 tablespoons	30 ml	canola oil
4 tablespoons	60 ml	flour
4 teaspoons	20 ml	white sugar
1 teaspoon	5 ml	soy sauce
1/2 cup	120 ml	water

Trim any fat from the meat. Cut the roast into 1/2- to 3/4-inch-thick slices. Coat each slice of meat with mustard. Sprinkle lightly with salt and pepper. Place the meat in a large jar or deep glass dish with a lid. Refrigerate the meat while preparing the marinade.

Combine the onions, vinegar, water, cloves, bay leaves, peppercorns, and sugar in a small saucepan. Heat and stir until the sugar dissolves. Remove from the heat to cool.

Pour the cooled marinade over the meat. Cover the dish. Set the meat back in the refrigerator to marinate for 3 or 4 days. Turn the meat once daily while it marinates.

Pour the oil into a deep frying pan and heat it to medium-high. Remove the meat from the marinade, reserving the marinade. Brown the meat on both sides in the oil. Remove the frying pan from the heat. Remove the meat from the frying pan and set aside.

Add the flour to the drippings in the frying pan. If the pan is too dry to moisten the flour, add 1 additional teaspoon of oil. Stir the flour into the drippings until all of the moisture has been absorbed.

Slowly stir all of the marinade into the flour. Whisk until the flour is no longer lumpy. Remove the bay leaves.

Place the frying pan over medium-high heat. Cook and stir the marinade until it is a smooth gravy. Add the sugar, soy sauce, and water to the gravy. Stir well.

Strain the gravy and return it to the frying pan. Bring it to a boil and add the browned meat. Spoon the gravy around the meat. Decrease the heat to a slow boil. Cover the meat and cook for 1 to 1 1/2 hours, or until the meat is tender enough to cut with a fork. Stir the meat occasionally to prevent sticking. Serve.

Boca Grande Resident Suggests Iguana Stew

A narrow bridge separates the community of Boca Grande, on the Grande Barrier Island of Gasparilla off the southwest coast of Florida, from the hustle and bustle of the mainland. The seven-mile-long island has no high-rises and no traffic lights. A 104-year-old lighthouse looks down over a street with 80-year-old banyan trees, their multiple trunks suspended from high, overhead boughs. Quiet beaches of white sand stretch the entire Gulf of Mexico side of the island. The shore on the bay side is an expanse of rocks and mangroves, their roots several feet above the water line.

The locals love the place. It is also a haven for tourists, tarpon fishers, and iguanas that roam the island in numbers too large to count. The story is that iguanas were innocently introduced to Boca Grande over twenty years ago when a resident brought a mom and a pop, a prolific couple, back from a holiday. The lizard-like creatures are strict vegetarians, preferring a diet of leaves and flowers. With the serrated ridges on their backs and their crusty faces, they are not cuddly. They tuck themselves into turtle holes at night and sun themselves on the rocks in the warm afternoons.

Occasionally, the iguanas get under foot. A friend who lives in Boca Grande arrived home from a trip and discovered two of them, each about three feet in length, nestled against her front door. Incensed at their audacity to make themselves at home on her property, she charged right up to them, took them by their tails, and flung them from her deck.

She suggested we create an iguana stew. Here is our version.

Steak Tail Stew

(Serves 2 or 3)

1 pound	454 g	T-bone steak tails or stewing beef
2 tablespoons	30 ml	olive oil
1	1	large onion, cut into 8 wedges
¼ teaspoon	1.25 ml	salt
¼ teaspoon	1.25 ml	pepper
3	3	cloves garlic, thinly sliced
2 tablespoons	30 ml	capers
1	1	bay leaf
1 tablespoon	15 ml	chopped fresh parsley
1 cup	240 ml	dry white wine
2 tablespoons	30 ml	balsamic vinegar
1 cup	240 ml	whole baby carrots

Cut the steak tails into 1-inch chunks and trim away as much fat as possible.

Pour the olive oil into a heavy saucepan or deep frying pan.

Over medium heat, lightly brown the steak tails on all sides.

Add the onion wedges, salt, and pepper.

Decrease the heat to low, cover the pan, and cook the steak and onion for 20 minutes.

While this is cooking, mix together the garlic, capers, bay leaf, parsley, white wine, and balsamic vinegar.

Pour the wine mixture over the meat mixture.

Stir in the baby carrots. Cover the pan and simmer over low heat for 30 minutes.

Remove the lid and simmer, uncovered, for 30 minutes more. Serve.

Fry Bread Is a Gem in the Desert

Quartzsite, Arizona, is described as the gem and mineral capital of the world. It's also known as the largest gathering place of RVers. Every year, in January and February, hundreds of thousands of recreational vehicles congregate in Quartzsite. There are miles of flea markets where vendors sell just about anything a person could want. Although there are several campgrounds in the vicinity, most visitors choose to pick a cactus in the middle of the desert, park beside it, and call it home.

We arrived with full tanks of fuel, propane, and fresh water. Our holding tanks were empty, our generator was working, and our batteries were charged. As boondockers we had to survive without any hook-ups to water, electricity, cable TV, telephone, or sewer.

The Sonoran Desert surrounded us. Giant saguaro, prickly pear, cholla, barrel, and fuzzy hedgehog cacti dotted the brown landscape. Wind-swept pebbles covered the sand. We hiked along waterless riverbeds and dusty trails, found petroglyphs on rock faces, and avoided the numerous critters that live in holes around every scrubby bush.

We didn't find any rare gems in the desert, but we did discover and eat fry bread. It was so tasty that people lined up to buy it. After just one bite, we hurried back to our motorhome to create our version beside our favorite cactus.

Taco Fry Bread

(Serves 6)

2	2	loaves (1 pound each) frozen white bread dough
1½ pounds	680 g	lean ground beef
1¼ ounces	35 g	taco seasoning mix
¾ cup	180 ml	sour cream
¾ cup	180 ml	guacamole
2 cups	480 ml	shredded cheddar cheese
2 cups	480 ml	diced tomato
½ cup	120 ml	chopped green onion
2 cups	480 ml	shredded lettuce
2 cups	480 ml	salsa
¾ cup	180 ml	sliced black olives
1 cup	240 ml	canola oil

Set the bread dough out to defrost.

In a nonstick frying pan, stir the ground beef over medium-high heat until browned and thoroughly cooked. Drain away any excess fat.

Stir in the dry taco seasoning mix. Continue to cook and stir for 2 minutes and then remove the ground beef from the heat.

Place the sour cream, guacamole, cheese, tomato, onion, lettuce, salsa, and olives in individual dishes.

Cut each loaf of bread dough into thirds to make 6 equal portions.

Stretch and flatten each portion of the bread dough to about 6 by 6 inches (15 by 15 centimeters), trying to keep an even thickness.

Heat the canola oil in a deep, heavy frying pan over medium-high heat. Test the temperature of the oil with a small piece of dough. The oil should bubble gently when the dough goes in.

Fry one piece of dough at a time for about 2 minutes on each side. When the dough is a deep golden brown on the bottom side, grasp it with a pair of tongs and turn it over. When cooked, the dough should be golden brown on both sides, soft in the center, and easy to pull apart, like fresh bread.

Drain each piece of cooked fry bread by standing it on end on a piece of paper towel, between two coffee mugs. A dish rack works even better, but it can become greasy.

Reheat the ground beef.

Top each piece of fry bread with a layer of sour cream, guacamole, ground beef, cheese, tomato, onion, lettuce, salsa, and olives.

A Recipe a Person Can Bet On

The new Las Vegas, still a unique oasis in the middle of the Mojave Desert, is continually growing and constantly changing. When old hotels go down, colossal hotel complexes rise from the dust.

At the Paris Las Vegas, a two-thirds replica of the famous Parisian landmark the Arc de Triomphe stands at the entrance to the hotel. A fifty-story Eiffel Tower looms over the sidewalk cafés and gaming tables.

At the New York-New York Hotel, we strolled through Greenwich Village, which was authentic right down to the steam rising from the manhole covers.

The Luxor, the world's second largest hotel, is thirty-six stories high and shaped like an Egyptian pyramid. The ten-story tall Sphinx at the entrance to the hotel is taller than the original Sphinx. The light that shines from the top of the Luxor pyramid is the most powerful beam of light in the world.

At the entrance to the Mirage, a volcano spews smoke and fire. The sea battle outside Treasure Island is a free attraction for young and old. The Rio is known for its Masquerade Show in the Sky.

And, who would have guessed that a person could have a true Italian experience while visiting the casino capital of the world? There is no longer any need to go to Venice when the Venetian Hotel and Casino is in Las Vegas. It is complete with canals, gondolas, and singing gondoliers.

This rich braised pork dish is a recipe to bet on.

Braised Pork and Cabbage

(Serves 4 to 6)

2 tablespoons	30 ml	vegetable or olive oil
2 pounds	907 g	pork, cut into 1-inch cubes
1	1	medium onion, diced
2	2	cloves garlic, minced
4 cups	960 ml	chopped cabbage
1 cup	240 ml	water
¼ cup	60 ml	soy sauce
1 teaspoon	5 ml	ground ginger

Heat the oil over medium-high heat in a large, deep frying pan.

Add the raw cubed pork. Brown the pork lightly on all sides.

Remove the pork pieces from the pan. Add the diced onion, minced garlic, and chopped cabbage to the hot frying pan and stir for 3 minutes over medium-high heat.

Mix the water, soy sauce, and ground ginger together. Add to the frying pan.

Bring the liquid to a boil. Return the pork to the pan.

Turn the heat down to medium-low. Cover the pan.

Cook for 45 minutes, or until the pork is tender. Stir occasionally. Add a little water if the meat and cabbage mixture becomes too dry before the pork is tender. Serve.

New Recipes and New Roads Are Full of Surprises

We were on our way to watch the whales at Tadoussac, Quebec. Suddenly traffic stopped. Ahead of us, cars snaked out of sight around a bend in the road. We assumed it was either an accident or a construction zone. No problem. We were traveling in our motorhome. We could make ourselves a pot of tea. While we waited, we took photos of the morning fog creeping up from the fjord-like shore of the St. Lawrence River.

Traffic inched forward, and we discovered that we were about to board a ferry. What happened to Highway 138? In a panic we wondered what to do. A U-turn with sixty feet (eighteen meters) of combined motorhome and towed car was impossible. The road was narrow. There were no shoulders. We'd have to unhitch the car, stop traffic in both directions, and even then keep our fingers crossed that we wouldn't wipe out the upcoming information booth.

A man frantically motioned us onto the ferry. We were holding up traffic.

"How do we get to Highway 138?" we asked.

"The ferry is the highway," the man said.

The good news was that we didn't have to turn around. The exciting news was that we were about to cross the mouth of the Saguenay River and we were going in the right direction after all.

We weren't sure that combining apples with soy sauce in the following recipe was the right direction either, but when we sampled the final product, it was perfect.

Apple Pork Chops and Rice

(Serves 2)

2	2	cloves garlic
2	2	pork chops
1 teaspoon	5 ml	canola oil
1 cup	240 ml	canned sliced apples
½ cup	120 ml	water
1 tablespoon	15 ml	soy sauce
2	2	servings rice

Peel the garlic cloves. Peeling garlic cloves is easy if the cloves are placed on the counter top and smashed by covering them with a large knife, flat side down, and banging the flat knife blade with the heel of a hand.

Trim excess fat from the pork chops.

Place the oil and the garlic cloves in a frying pan and heat to medium-high.

Add the chops and brown them on both sides. When they are browned, cover them with the apple slices. Add the water and soy sauce. Turn the heat to low, cover the pan, and cook for 30 minutes.

Cook the rice according to the package's instructions.

When the pork chops are tender, transfer them to dinner plates and place a garlic clove on each chop. Cover each chop with apples. Place the rice beside the pork chop. Trickle sauce from the frying pan over the rice and serve.

Rome Wasn't Built in a Day, But Guthrie Was

When the sun rose on April 22, 1889, Guthrie, Oklahoma, consisted of a water tank, two houses, and a railway depot. In the early morning, Guthrie was alive with deputy U.S. marshals, judges, reporters, government officials, and eager settlers who were bold enough to arrive before the official start of the Oklahoma Land Rush. Anyone who entered the unassigned lands prior to noon was prohibited from making a land claim, but some eager land-grabbers, known as "sooners," didn't pay any attention to the law. Long before the first horseback rider galloped in from the east at 12:40, the sooners had claimed most of the valuable town lots.

The first of many trains arrived at 1:25. As each train slowed, land-hungry men and women jumped from the windows, cowcatchers, and roofs. They ran until they found a piece of land without a flag and drove in a stake bearing their names or initials. Those with bicycles and buggies were able to push further afield to the 160-acre home-steads. By nightfall, there were ten to fifteen thousand people living in Guthrie.

On that first night in Guthrie, on their own land, few people had either a roof over their heads, a bed under their bodies, or a good meal in their stomachs. What a luxury these pork chops would have been. And you can bet your land claim that those early-bird sooners would have been first in line for the grub.

Lemon–Red Currant Pork Chops

(Serves 2)

4	4	*thin boneless center-cut pork loin chops*
1 teaspoon	5 ml	*freshly squeezed lemon juice*
1 tablespoon	15 ml	*red currant jelly*
½ teaspoon	2.5 ml	*prepared mustard*
1 teaspoon	5 ml	*capers*
		nonstick cooking spray

Trim any visible fat from the chops.

Combine the lemon juice, red currant jam, mustard, and capers in a small bowl.

Lightly spray a nonstick frying pan with cooking oil spray.

Heat the frying pan to medium-high and brown the chops lightly on both sides, for about 30 seconds per side.

Spread the red currant mixture evenly over the pork chops and cover tightly. Reduce the heat to medium-low and cook for 15 minutes, or until the chops are tender.

Place the pork chops on a serving dish. Stir the red currant sauce in the frying pan and pour it over the pork chops. Serve.

Shakespeare's Hamlet Leads to Pork Recipe

Happy as swans, we spent an entire week in Stratford, Ontario, immersing ourselves in the theatre, the food, and the scenery. We ate three-course picnics beside the Avon River, prepared by the chefs of the Festival Theatre's Greenroom. We tried on costumes during a tour of the costume warehouse and attended plays at the Avon, Tom Patterson, and Festival Theatres.

We were inspired during Hamlet's famous soliloquy in Act III, Scene I, which contains the line, "Ay, there's the rub." The quotation has nothing to do with cooking. Hamlet meant, "Yes, there's the snag." But that didn't stop us from thinking about recipes. In the culinary sense, a rub is a form of seasoning.

Stratford offers its residents and visitors a blend of the past and the present. Shakespeare's themes of love and revenge are as prevalent today as they were almost four hundred years ago. But, just the same, who would have guessed that, in the early 1600s, when Shakespeare wrote Hamlet, his famous narration would lead to this culinary creation?

Lemon-Rubbed Pork Chops

(Serves 4)

¼	¼	lemon
4	4	pork chops
1 teaspoon	5 ml	canola oil
2 cups	480 ml	apple juice
1	1	onion, thinly sliced
2 tablespoons	30 ml	finely chopped parsley
¼ teaspoon	1.25 ml	dry ground basil
2 teaspoons	10 ml	cornstarch
4 teaspoons	20 ml	water
¼ teaspoon	1.25 ml	salt
¼ teaspoon	1.25 ml	black pepper

Rub the lemon over both sides of the pork chops.

Chop the lemon, including the rind, and set it aside.

Heat the oil in a deep frying pan. Add the pork chops and brown on both sides.

Pour the apple juice over the pork chops and add the chopped lemon, onion slices, chopped parsley, and ground basil.

Cover the pan and cook the chops over medium-low heat for 35 to 45 minutes, or until the meat is tender.

Transfer the meat to a serving dish and cover to keep warm. Continue to cook the onion and lemon in the frying pan.

In a small bowl, combine the cornstarch and water and add it to the apple juice, lemon, and onion. Stir well and add the salt and pepper.

When the mixture has thickened, pour it over the pork chops and serve.

A Morsel of What to Sample in Texas Hill Country

In the late afternoon we pulled into the Fredericksburg, Texas, KOA campground in the heart of Texas Hill Country. We unhitched the car from the motorhome and went to the office to collect maps and brochures about the area. We decided to seek out the Wildseed Farms, the Pacific War Museums, and the best German restaurant in town. We were leaving the next day and we knew we didn't have time for the Wine Trail, the Herb Farm, the Pioneer Museum, the historical German church, the Cowboy Artists of America Museum, LBJ's Ranch, nearby Luckenbach, or Johnson City, the boyhood home of former president Lyndon B. Johnson. Climbing the summit of Enchanted Rock and enjoying the spectacular view of the Texas Hill Country would have to wait for another visit.

At the Wildseed Farms, we walked along the rows of bluebonnets and poppies. Years ago, it was Lady Bird Johnson who, as a neighbor to the Wildseed Farms, worked with the owners to have the seeds strewn along the shoulders of Texas state highways. Today, the roadside ditches are ablaze with color.

At the Pacific War Museums, we managed to see most of the exhibits before the curator locked us out. We finished the day with hot German potato salad, red cabbage, pork schnitzel, and dark beer at Der Lindenbaum Restaurant.

The German heritage of Fredericksburg is very evident, not only in the food, but also in the architecture and the names on mailboxes and tombstones.

This is the pork schnitzel recipe we served in our restaurants for many years.

Tender Pork Schnitzel

(Serves 3)

6	6	boneless center-cut fast-fry pork loin chops
½ cup	120 ml	flour
½ teaspoon	2.5 ml	salt
½ teaspoon	2.5 ml	black pepper
1	1	egg
½ cup	120 ml	milk
1 cup	240 ml	bread crumbs
6 tablespoons	90 ml	canola oil
		lemon wedges
		parsley

Trim any excess fat from the pork chops.

Pound each pork chop to make it thinner. Before pounding, place a plastic bag over the meat to prevent splattering. Pound the pork with a meat pounder until the chops are flattened to about twice their original size and the thickness is consistent over the entire chop.

Place the flour, salt, and pepper in a bowl and mix well. Break the egg into a second bowl and whisk. Add the milk and whisk again until the egg and milk are completely blended. Place the bread crumbs in a third bowl.

Take a pounded schnitzel and dip it into the flour. Cover the meat completely with flour then lift it out while shaking away any excess. Dip the schnitzel into the egg mixture. Cover the meat completely, then lift it out slowly to allow the excess to drip off. Dip the schnitzel into the bread crumbs. Cover the schnitzel entirely, then lift it out and shake away any excess. Place the breaded schnitzel on a plate and follow the same procedure with the remaining schnitzels.

Heat the oil over medium-low in a large frying pan. The secret to tenderness is slow cooking on a low heat. Allow the oil to heat for 2 minutes. Place the breaded schnitzels in the frying pan. When they begin to bubble slowly, cook the schnitzels for 2 to 3 minutes on each side, or until the breading becomes golden brown.

Remove the schnitzels from the frying pan and blot both sides with paper towel to remove greasiness. Arrange the schnitzels on a serving dish and garnish with lemon wedges and parsley sprigs.

Louisiana's Cajun and Creole Cuisine

The first French colonists arrived in Acadia in 1604. In 1621, the English government changed the name of Acadia to Nova Scotia. Control of the area passed back and forth between France and England several times. In 1749, England demanded an unconditional oath of allegiance from the Acadians. However, the Acadians wished to remain neutral and not take up arms against either England or France. As a result, in 1755, most of the Acadians were deported from Nova Scotia and the British confiscated their farms. Many moved to the predominantly French territory and bayou country of Louisiana, and the term Cajun, a corrupted word for Acadian, was born.

Cajun food is traditionally cooked with all the ingredients together in a black iron pot. The heavy pot keeps the contents from sticking. Jambalaya is an example of a one-pot Cajun meal.

The Creole influence in Louisiana was different. The Creoles were the European born aristocrats wooed by the Spanish to establish New Orleans. The Spanish influence gave Creole food its spice.

While both cuisines are somewhat distinct, both the Creoles and Cajuns agree that there is no single rule and no single recipe when it comes to the matters of food. Have fun with the jambalaya. Add shrimp, ham, chicken, leftover turkey, sausage, or even alligator, which the early Cajun trappers considered quite tasty.

Jambalaya

(Serves 3)

1 tablespoon	15 ml	minced onion flakes
1 tablespoon	15 ml	garlic salt
½ tablespoon	7.5 ml	dried oregano leaves
½ tablespoon	7.5 ml	dried sweet basil
½ teaspoon	2.5 ml	dried thyme
½ teaspoon	2.5 ml	black pepper
¼ teaspoon	1.25 ml	dry red pepper flakes
½ teaspoon	2.5 ml	cayenne pepper
2½ teaspoons	12.5 ml	sweet paprika
1	1	large skinless, boneless chicken breast
4 teaspoons	20 ml	canola oil
12 ounces	340 g	smoked sausage
		nonstick cooking spray
½	½	large onion, coarsely chopped
½	½	large green pepper, cubed
2	2	cloves garlic, finely chopped
2	2	celery stalks, chopped
1	1	small can tomato paste
14 ounces	420 ml	whole or diced tomatoes with liquid
1½ cups	360 ml	water
1	1	chicken bouillon cube
1½ cups	360 ml	long-grain rice, cooked

To make the Creole seasoning, combine the onion flakes, garlic salt, oregano, basil, thyme, black pepper, red pepper flakes, cayenne, and paprika. Set aside.

Cut the chicken breast into bite-sized pieces. In a frying pan, heat 1 teaspoon of the canola oil to medium-high and brown the chicken. Sprinkle the chicken with a little of the Creole seasoning. Remove the chicken from the heat and set aside.

Cut the sausage into bite-sized pieces. Spray a frying pan with nonstick cooking spray and heat to medium-high. Brown the sausage. Set aside.

Heat the remaining 3 teaspoons canola oil in a large pot over medium-high heat. Cook and stir the onion, green pepper, garlic, and celery until the onions are translucent. Add the chicken, sausage, tomato paste, tomatoes, water, bouillon cube, and 2 tablespoons of Creole seasoning. Stir to dissolve the bouillon cube. Cook for 10 minutes. Turn the heat to medium-low. Add the cooked rice. Cook for 10 minutes, stirring gently so it doesn't stick. If the jambalaya has too much liquid, cook it a little longer. If it is too thick, add a little water. Serve. (Save leftover Creole seasoning for another use.)

Cod Caught by Camera

The captain and his first mate offered us raincoats as the *Greenwitch* passed beyond the sand dunes that protect the harbor of Stanley Bridge, Prince Edward Island. We declined. It was a clear, sunny morning and we were after cod.

"People interested in relaxing and suntanning go out after lunch," Susan Graham of Graham's Deep Sea Fishing told us. We chose to go to sea early, when the fish bite.

The wind and the size of the waves picked up as soon as we were out in the open water. The first mate was wearing a bright yellow raincoat. Great sprays of salt water drenched our hair and clothes.

When we reached the best spot for catching cod, the captain cut the engine. The boat still bobbed up and down in the water, but we didn't notice. We didn't even notice our wet clothes. We were too busy listening to instructions as the captain baited our lines with bar clams. "Let your line out until it hits the bottom, then turn the line back five turns on the reel and wait."

Within seconds Phyllis yelled, "Get the camera ready." The tip of her pole bent toward the water. Without much of a fight, she reeled in a shiny, smooth, flipping cod. The captain removed the fish and re-baited her hook. Again, Phyllis tossed out her line.

"Get the camera," she said.

Fifteen pictures of cod later, the captain turned the *Greenwitch* to shore. The first mate filleted the fish as we road the waves in the direction of Stanley Harbour. On the return trip, having learned our lesson, we were dressed in bright yellow raincoats.

Crispy Cod à l'Orange

(Serves 4)

1	1	red pepper, seeded and cut into very thin strips
1	1	sweet onion, thinly sliced
2 tablespoons	30 ml	fresh orange juice
1	1	large clove garlic, minced
¼ teaspoon	1.25 ml	salt
¼ teaspoon	1.25 ml	pepper
1 pound	454 g	cod fillets
		all-purpose flour
4 tablespoons	60 ml	canola oil
2 tablespoons	30 ml	grated orange zest

Combine the red pepper, onion, orange juice, garlic, salt, and pepper in a bowl.

Pat the cod fillets dry with a paper towel and dust lightly with flour.

Heat the canola oil in a large frying pan until hot. Add the cod to the hot oil and sprinkle 1 tablespoon of the grated orange peel over the cod.

Fry the cod until crispy and golden brown on one side. Turn the cod over and sprinkle the remaining 1 tablespoon orange peel over the cod. Add a little extra canola oil to the pan, if necessary, to prevent sticking.

Cover the cod with the red pepper and onion mixture. Steam the vegetables on top of the cod for about 5 minutes, or until the cod is crispy on the bottom side.

With a spatula, transfer the cod and vegetables from the pan to a serving plate.

Floundering in a Canoe
Is Picture Perfect

Norm Bullock lives on the north coast of Vancouver Island. Whenever he gets a chance, Norm escapes to his private camp on a secluded pebble beach and lives like Robinson Crusoe. The large driftwood chair under his lean-to gives him a view of the water and any approaching bear from down the beach. He goes fishing in a canoe.

Phyllis and Norm set out in the canoe to catch halibut. Norm said that he once caught a two-hundred-pounder. Phyllis was certain that a two-hundred-pound halibut would pull the canoe all the way to Alaska. She handed her fishing pole to Norm. He caught three flounder and suggested they go ashore for lunch. With her mind still on the possibility of being pulled to Alaska, Phyllis thought going to shore was a really good idea.

After lunch, Norm and Lamont set out to see what they could catch. The waters of Broughton Strait were calm. Across the channel, the red roof of Pultnay Point Lighthouse marked the beginning of the enormous Queen Charlotte Strait. After dropping the line to the bottom several times, Lamont caught a flounder. Norm pointed to something behind Lamont. She turned to see a cruise ship the size of several football fields coming toward them.

"It'll take five minutes for it to get here and three minutes for us to reach shore," Norm said. Lamont and Norm paddled quickly. They were less than a minute from shore when Phyllis waved Lamont and Norm back in the direction of the cruise ship.

"Stop," she yelled as she raised her camera. "This is a great shot."

Normally, Norm steams his flounder between the hot rocks of an outdoor fire pit. Our method can be done in a kitchen.

Sesame Steamed Flounder

(Serves 3)

4	4	leeks, white part only
⅓ cup	80 ml	water
⅓ cup	80 ml	white wine
1 tablespoon	15 ml	sesame oil
13 ounces	369 g	flounder or sole
		salt
		pepper
½ teaspoon	2.5 ml	ground ginger

Cut the white part of the leeks into thin rounds. Break the rounds into rings. Wash the leek rings well because they are often gritty.

Spread the leek rings over the bottom of a deep frying pan.

Combine the water, wine, and sesame oil. Stir to mix thoroughly. Pour the liquid over the leeks.

Bring the liquid to a boil then turn the heat to medium-low.

Place the flounder fillets in a single layer on top of the leeks.

Sprinkle salt and pepper over the flounder fillets.

Cover the pan and steam the fish for 2 to 3 minutes. Test the flounder for doneness.

Transfer the flounder to serving dishes.

Add the ginger to the leeks and stir well.

Spoon the leeks over the flounder and serve.

Pull Up These Socks and Get Mussels

When the lobster season is over on the north shore of Prince Edward Island, some lobster fishers scrub down their boats and join the harbor cruise business. As tour guides, they take tourists out past the sand dunes, the lighthouses, and the red limestone bluffs into the choppy waters of the Gulf of St. Lawrence.

On our tour we passed numerous long rows of white, orange, and green floats that dotted the surface of the water and looked like swimming lanes in an Olympic pool. Between the floats, cultivated mussels grow in plastic mesh socks that dangle from long lines suspended in the water. These cultivated mussels tend to be free of predators like starfish and crabs, as well as irritants like sand and grit from the sandy bottom of the water.

Cultivated mussels are available year round. We heard tales of how the mussel farmers have to cut through the winter ice with chain saws in order to pull up their socks of mature twelve- to eighteen-month-old mussels.

Part of the harbor cruise experience was a sunset and a feast of mussels steamed in their own juices. For our mussel recipe, we created a liquid that combines several flavors that not only complement the mussels but also make a great dipping broth for freshly baked bread.

Steamed Mussels

(Serves 2 or 3)

½	½	onion, finely diced
¼	¼	lemon (rind and flesh), finely chopped
1	1	tomato, finely diced
2	2	cloves garlic, minced
¼ teaspoon	1.25 ml	dried basil
1 cup	240 ml	water
½ teaspoon	2.5 ml	hot sauce
3 pounds	1.36 kg	mussels
1	1	baguette, sliced

Combine the onion, lemon, tomato, garlic, basil, water, and hot sauce in a large, deep pot and bring to a boil.

Rinse the mussels under cold water. Discard any mussels that are not tightly closed.

Add the mussels to the boiling mixture. Turn the heat to medium, cover the pot, and steam the mussels for about 8 minutes, or until the shells are wide open and the meat is coming loose from the shell. Stir once by gently lifting the bottom mussels to the top.

Place the mussels in large bowls. Discard any mussels that have not opened during the cooking process. Pour the hot broth over the mussels.

Garnish the bowls with parsley and lemon.

Serve the mussels with sliced baguette for dipping.

The Bear Facts about Hyder, Alaska

The Stewart-Cassiar Highway, Highway 37 North, travels 450 miles (725 kilometers) through northern British Columbia to the Yukon border. An alternative to the British Columbia portion of the Alaska Highway, it is pavement with gravel stretches and one-lane bridges.

One of the best reasons to drive the Stewart-Cassiar is the side trip on Highway 37A to the twin communities of Stewart, British Columbia, and Hyder, Alaska. En route, we passed snowcapped mountains and hanging glaciers. We drove within yards of Bear Glacier and watched as glacier calves broke away from the mother glacier and bobbed in the cold, ice-blue water.

Stewart is known for its neat-as-a-pin Canadian tidiness and Hyder for its end-of-the-road Alaskan character. The road on the Canadian side of the international border is paved. The road on the Alaskan side is dust with potholes. Stewart has a population of eight hundred. It is a typical North American small town with stores, schools, and houses along organized streets and avenues. Hyder, population sixty, is a haphazard assortment of log cabins, run-down shacks, tired trucks, and transient recreational vehicles.

The lure of Hyder is the Fish Creek Wildlife Viewing Area, just a short drive out of town. In July and August, brown and black bears hang out at Fish Creek to eat the spawning chum salmon. The local rangers built a boardwalk along the creek so that visitors can safely observe the bears as they fish. We watched several grizzlies and a black bear scoop salmon out of the water.

Moist Mayo Poached Salmon

(Serves 2 or 3)

6 tablespoons	90 ml	mayonnaise
½ cup	120 ml	white wine
4 tablespoons	60 ml	finely diced onion
2 teaspoons	10 ml	drained capers, plus more for garnish
1 pound	454 g	salmon fillet
		parsley

Combine the mayonnaise and wine in a small bowl and whisk until smooth. Add the diced onion and capers and stir well.

Place the mayonnaise mixture in a deep frying pan and heat the mixture until it is bubbling softly. Turn the heat to medium-low.

Place the salmon on top of the mayonnaise mixture, with the skin side down and flesh up. Cover the pan.

Poach the salmon for about 20 minutes, or until the flesh is no longer translucent. Occasionally spoon the mayonnaise mixture over the salmon.

Remove the salmon to a serving dish. Garnish with capers, fresh parsley, and a little of the poaching sauce and serve. Leftovers make excellent salmon sandwiches.

Catching Low Tide on the Gaspé

It is difficult to miss Percé Rock, one of the most recognized natural attractions in Canada. Once attached to the shoreline, it rises abruptly out of the water of the Gulf of St. Lawrence, along the eastern shore of the Gaspé Peninsula in the province of Quebec. The name is derived from the fact that the sea has pierced holes in the giant rock structure, forming archways. In recent times, a single, large arched opening pierces the 1,420-foot-long (433 meters) and 288-foot-high (88 meters) stone block. Throughout the day the light, the tide and the weather dramatically change the rock's appearance. Hundreds of tons of pebbles crumble away from the edifice into the sea each year.

At low tide, we walked the sandy beach and the exposed pebbled ridge that curves all the way out to Percé Rock. The safest time to do this is an hour before or an hour after low tide. The arch can be reached by walking through a slippery rock pool. Later, at high tide, we climbed the bluff overlooking Percé Rock. It was eerie to see that the Gulf of St. Lawrence flowed where we had recently walked.

Percé Rock is a bird sanctuary, home to the northern gannet. The gannet, a large, long-winged seabird, catches its dinner by plunge-diving from great heights into the cold seawater. Fish and squid are the bird's main diet. Scallops are safe from the gannet's tapered beak.

Curried Scallops and Vegetables

(Serves 2 or 3)

2 cups	480 ml	chopped cabbage
10 to 12	10 to 12	large sea scallops
2 tablespoons	30 ml	canola oil
1 tablespoon	15 ml	minced garlic
1 tablespoon	15 ml	minced ginger
¾ cup	180 ml	finely diced onion
¼ cup	60 ml	finely chopped carrot
1	1	chicken bouillon cube
1 teaspoon	5 ml	curry powder
1 cup	240 ml	frozen peas
1 cup	240 ml	frozen French-style green beans

Put the chopped cabbage in a saucepan and almost cover it with water. Cook the cabbage until it softens but still has firmness. Drain the cabbage and reserve the juice in a separate container.

Wash the scallops, pat them dry with a paper towel, and set them aside.

In a large, deep frying pan, heat the oil to medium-high and add the garlic, ginger, onion, and carrot. Combine the flavors by stirring for 2 to 3 minutes, or until the carrot begins to soften but still has firmness.

Add the bouillon cube and ³/₄ cup of the reserved cabbage broth to the frying pan. Stir constantly to dissolve the bouillon cube. When the bouillon cube is dissolved, add the curry powder and continue to cook for 3 minutes.

Add the partially cooked cabbage. When the mixture bubbles, add the frozen peas, frozen beans, and scallops. Stir constantly for 2 to 3 minutes to heat the peas and beans and to cook the scallops. Do not overcook the scallops; the moment they are no longer translucent they are done. Serve immediately.

Fishing Made Easy

The Thunderbird RV Park in Campbell River, British Columbia, is run by the Campbell River First Nations. From the RV park, we could walk across the road, sit on the beach, and watch cruise ships and Orca whales go by. When someone sights a whale, they hurry to the office to ring the cowbell and yell, "The killer whales are here." As for fishing, we could cast our line off the wharf or buy fresh salmon from a local fish market.

We discovered that the quickest way to get sockeye salmon, prawns, crab, snapper, halibut, and shrimp out of the water and into our tummies was to go to the fish shop and see Bob. Bob and his wife, Pat, own Patti Finn's Seafood, a fish shop located on the dock at the Discovery Bay Marina in Campbell River. The marina was overflowing with large personal yachts whenever we dropped by to pick up the fresh catch of the day. The largest yacht was 115 feet (35 meters) long.

Bob Martin and his son, John, gave us a tour of their prawn boat, the *September Isle*. It was tied up at Fisherman's Wharf. The *September Isle* was equipped to catch, freeze, and package prawns for the Japanese market. When full, the boat held six thousand pounds of frozen prawns.

Prawns are very similar to shrimp. Unlike other seafood, prawns are not farmed or artificially cultivated. The British Columbia Spot Prawn is the most prized in the world. According to Bob, the cold coastal water makes the prawn flesh firmer and the taste sweeter.

When the *September Isle* is at sea, John is the designated cook for the crew. He shared this shrimp recipe with us.

Shrimp in Beer Batter

(Serves 3 or 4)

30	30	*medium to large shrimp or prawns*
3 cups	*720 ml*	*canola oil*
1 cup	*240 ml*	*dry pancake mix*
½ cup	*120 ml*	*beer*
1 teaspoon	*5 ml*	*lemon-pepper seasoning*

Peel and devein the shrimp, leaving the tails attached.

Place the oil in a wok, deep fryer, or deep frying pan.

In a bowl, whisk the dry pancake mix with the beer and lemon-pepper seasoning until the mixture is smooth.

Heat the oil until just bubbling.

Pat the shrimp dry with a paper towel. Hold each shrimp by the tail and dip it into the batter. Carefully drop each shrimp into the hot oil. The oil should be hot enough to bubble but not spit as a shrimp is dropped.

Turn each shrimp over when it turns golden brown and floats to the surface.

Lift the browned floating shrimp onto a paper towel to remove any grease before serving.

Serve the shrimp by themselves or with a shrimp cocktail sauce.

Alert Bay Is Worth the Wait for the Ferry

According to locals, the ferry from Port McNeill, British Columbia, on the north end of Vancouver Island, to Alert Bay, on Cormorant Island, is always late. Whatever the reason, we are grateful. The day we took the fifteen-minute ferry ride, as foot passengers, we would never have seen as much of the island had the ferry been on time for the return trip. We wouldn't have seen the home of John Ingraham, the painter and carver. A giant whale rises out of his front lawn. We would not have seen the totem poles in the old cemetery or the world's tallest totem pole beside the Big House. In fact, we would not have had time to see all the exhibits in the U'Mista Cultural Centre, and Andrea, the curator, would not have had time to drive us around the town.

In the U'Mista Cultural Centre, Andrea's sister, Lillian, explained the songs and dances of the masks and the thin shield-shaped copper pieces of the Potlatch Ceremony of the Kwakwaka'wakw First Nations. When potlatch gatherings were made illegal in 1884, the First Nations people were no longer allowed to practice their culture. The Canadian government and private collectors confiscated masks and other ceremonial gear. Since the lifting of the cultural ban in 1950 some, but not all, of the treasures have been returned to the Cultural Centre.

Island residents know that the Alert Bay ferry is always late so they continue about their business until they see it coming across the water. As the ferry enters the harbor, they make their way to the dock.

The ferry was an hour late the day we went to Alert Bay, just long enough for a person to cook this shrimp ratatouille recipe and still catch a ride back to the mainland.

Shrimp Ratatouille

(Serves 6 to 8)

1	1	medium eggplant
		salt
3	3	onions
2	2	green peppers
¾ pound	340 g	mushrooms
3	3	small zucchini
3	3	cloves garlic, minced
6 tablespoons	90 ml	canola oil
½ teaspoon	2.5 ml	tarragon
½ teaspoon	2.5 ml	mint
½ teaspoon	2.5 ml	dill weed
½ teaspoon	2.5 ml	black pepper
¾ cup	180 ml	red wine
48 ounces	1440 ml	canned crushed tomatoes
1¼ pounds	567 g	medium shrimp, raw or cooked
1 tablespoon	15 ml	canola oil
1 teaspoon	5 ml	garlic salt
		grated cheddar cheese

Peel and cut the eggplant into 1-inch pieces. Place them in a bowl, sprinkle them with salt and let them stand for about 20 minutes. Rinse thoroughly and set aside.

Cut the onions into eighths. Cut the green peppers into 1-inch pieces. Cut the mushrooms into halves or quarters in order to match the size of the other vegetables (button mushrooms can be used whole).

Trim the ends from the zucchini and cut them into ½-inch rounds. Keep the zucchini separate from the other vegetables.

In a large saucepan, heat the oil then slowly cook the onions, garlic, peppers, and mushrooms for 5 minutes, or until just beginning to soften. Stir constantly.

Add the tarragon, mint, dill weed, black pepper, red wine, zucchini, and eggplant. Cover the saucepan and cook over medium heat for 5 minutes.

Stir in the crushed tomatoes. Cook for 30 minutes. Stir occasionally.

If using raw shrimp, peel, devein, wash, and place in paper towels to dry thoroughly. Heat the oil in a nonstick frying pan over medium-high. Stir in the garlic salt. Add the shrimp. Toss and stir the shrimp for about 1 minute, or until they just turn orange. Immediately remove the shrimp from the pan to prevent them from overcooking.

Add the cooked shrimp to the ratatouille. Stir and cook for about 1 minute.

Transfer the ratatouille to a serving bowl and sprinkle grated cheese over the top. Serve extra grated cheese on the side. This dish is perfect over rice.

Tuning in to Chautauqua

The Chautauqua Institution in Chautauqua, New York, is a community that exists because its residents and visitors appreciate the community's founding principle. They support the idea that people have a right to be all that they can be, know all they can know, and do all they can do, providing they do not inhibit the rights of others in the process.

Chautauqua is like a giant feast where diners are invited to sit at the table, marvel at all that is before them, and sample the smorgasbord of churches, music, art, ballet, plays, and lectures.

Whenever friends invite us to their cottage in Chautauqua, the cultural feast is spread before us. And at the end of each day, on their front porch, we gorge ourselves with warm conversation and culinary delights.

We always come away from Chautauqua with a renewed appreciation for life and friendship. Sometimes our hostess prepares her special grilled tuna recipe. Rather than grilled, our version is seared quickly in a frying pan.

Marinated Tuna Steaks with Dipping Sauce

(Serves 2)

1 cup	240 ml	apple juice
½ teaspoon	2.5 ml	ground ginger
4 teaspoons	20 ml	hoisin sauce
1 teaspoon	5 ml	soy sauce
¼ teaspoon	1.25 ml	garlic salt
½ teaspoon	2.5 ml	wasabi horseradish
2	2	tuna steaks
		nonstick cooking oil

To make the marinade, put the apple juice, ginger, hoisin sauce, soy sauce, garlic salt, and wasabi in a small bowl. Whisk thoroughly to combine.

Wash the tuna steaks. Pat them dry with a paper towel. Place the tuna steaks in a deep dish. Pour 6 tablespoons of the marinade over the tuna steaks. Seal the container and refrigerate for 15 minutes. Turn the steaks over and refrigerate for 15 minutes more.

Place the remaining marinade in a saucepan. Bring it to a boil then decrease the heat to a slow boil. Cook for at least 15 minutes. When the marinade begins to thicken, remove it from the heat and set aside.

Heat a frying pan to medium-high. Spray the pan lightly with nonstick cooking oil.

Fry the tuna steaks 2 minutes on each side.

Reheat the marinade.

Place the tuna steaks on serving plates and serve them with a side dish of warmed marinade for dipping.

Trees Along the Icefield Parkway Resemble Asparagus

In local grocery stores, fresh asparagus is available in bunches held together by purple elastic bands. If one were to take several bunches, remove the elastic, and stand the asparagus spears up on their own, they would look just like the evergreen trees growing in dense thickets along the Icefield Parkway between Banff and the Columbia Icefields in Alberta. The trees are straight and very spindly, with no lower branches.

Farther up the parkway, the Icefield Centre that coordinates tours to the Athabaska Glacier is located in a sub-alpine climate. There, at an altitude of six thousand feet, in contrast to the asparagus forest, the shorter, even more stunted trees are three hundred years old. Looking more like overgrown Japanese bonsai trees, their branches grow only on one side. The wind gives them this "flagged" design.

On the surrounding mountains, above the tree line, there are no trees at all. Only low-lying plants are able to survive. On the other hand, mountain goats thrive. We learned that they climb down to the highway in winter and early spring to lick the salt that the road crews spread to melt the ice. The salt probably adds a little zing to their spindly mountain rations just like the flavors in this recipe add zing to fresh asparagus.

Asparagus Oriental

(Serves 4 or 5)

1 teaspoon	5 ml	sesame oil
2 tablespoons	30 ml	ginger marmalade
4	4	green onions, white and light green part only, thinly sliced
¼ cup	60 ml	sake
1 tablespoon	15 ml	light soy sauce
2 tablespoons	30 ml	hoisin sauce
½ cup	120 ml	sliced and julienned pickled beets
1 cup	240 ml	shredded carrot
32	32	fresh asparagus spears, tough ends removed

Heat the sesame oil in a wok or large frying pan over medium heat for 30 seconds.

Add the ginger marmalade and green onions. Stir fry for 2 minutes.

Add the sake, soy sauce, hoisin sauce, pickled beets, and shredded carrots. Stir fry for 2 minutes.

Spread the asparagus spears evenly over the mixture in the pan. Allow to steam for 7 minutes, stirring once or twice, or until each asparagus spear has turned a bright green color.

With tongs, transfer the asparagus spears from the pan to a serving platter.

Continue cooking and stirring the carrots and beets in the pan for about 3 minutes, or until the liquid has almost evaporated.

Spoon the hot mixture over the asparagus and serve.

How to Catch the Elusive Moose

On our 10,500-mile (17,000-kilometer) round trip from Mitchell, Ontario, to Tuktoyaktuk, Northwest Territories, we saw seventeen bears, two deer, six Dall sheep, one timber wolf, one red fox, two marmots, seventeen elk, one bison, eight caribou, nine Stone sheep, and one little moose. We saw her as we drove south on the Alaska Highway. She was licking salt from the gravel on the side of the road.

At Two Moose Lake on the Dempster Highway we followed moose tracks and searched the shoreline with our binoculars. People who pulled into a scenic rest area just behind us in the Ogilvie Mountains bragged about a large bull moose that had walked across the highway in front of their vehicle only minutes earlier. A mother and baby moose frequented the lake at Mountain Shadow campground along the Stewart-Cassiar Highway in Iskut, in northern British Columbia. But not while we were there. In Whitehorse, Yukon, we met the manager of a bank who found it hard to believe that we hadn't seen dozens of moose. She gave us a package of ground moose meat.

Finally, in Dryden, Ontario, we saw the world's biggest moose. Its name was Maximillion. It was a sculpture that stood over eighteen feet (five meters) high.

Perhaps we should have used this cabbage recipe as bait to catch the real thing.

Feta Creamed Cabbage

(Serves 4 to 6)

1	1	small cabbage, chopped
½ cup	120 ml	onion, finely chopped
2	2	cloves garlic, minced
1 tablespoon	15 ml	canola oil
3 tablespoons	45 ml	flour
1½ cups	360 ml	skim milk
½ teaspoon	2.5 ml	Worcestershire sauce
¼ teaspoon	1.25 ml	salt
½ teaspoon	2.5 ml	pepper
½ cup	120 ml	crumbled feta cheese

Boil the cabbage until tender. Drain well and set aside.

In a large saucepan, sauté the onion and garlic in the canola oil until the onions are translucent. Remove the saucepan from the heat. Add the flour. Mix until smooth.

Using a whisk, slowly blend in the milk. Add the Worcestershire sauce, salt, and pepper.

Place the saucepan over medium heat. Cook, stirring constantly, until the sauce thickens and the flour tastes cooked.

Stir in the feta cheese and whisk until thoroughly mixed.

Drain any accumulated water from the cabbage. Add the cabbage to the sauce. Stir to coat and heat the cabbage. Transfer to bowls and serve.

There Is Always the Potluck

In the RV world, where a new adventure waits around each bend in the road, there is one tradition that we can count on: the potluck. The social gathering where everyone contributes one dish to a meal is usually the best and biggest at Thanksgiving. Tables overflow with turkey, mashed potatoes, gravy, glazed sweet potatoes, sweet potato casserole, turnip, pumpkin, green bean casserole, brussels sprouts, candied carrots, cranberry mousse, cabbage, ham, oyster dressing, broad beans, Waldorf salad, marshmallow salad, mousse, pineapple fluff, cherry cake, chocolate cake, apple cake, cream puffs, coffee, tea, and lemonade.

Some years, we have two Thanksgiving dinners—a Canadian feast in October and an American spread in November.

When it comes to potluck contributions, we find that this carrot dish is easy to make and quickly gobbled up.

(Note that when preparing this dish for a crowd, you only need to increase the ginger, garlic, and bouillon cube by half of the other ingredients. For example, multiply everything by six and the ginger, garlic, and bouillon cube by three.)

Candied Carrots

(Serves 4)

2 tablespoons	30 ml	canola oil
4 tablespoons	60 ml	diced red onion
2 cups	480 ml	fresh baby carrots or carrot coins
1 teaspoon	5 ml	ground ginger
1 teaspoon	5 ml	garlic salt
2 tablespoons	30 ml	brown sugar
1	1	chicken bouillon cube
1 cup	240 ml	water

Place the canola oil in a frying pan over medium heat. Sauté the onions and carrots, stirring, for 3 minutes.

Add the ginger, garlic salt, and brown sugar to the carrots. Stir while cooking for 2 minutes.

Dissolve the bouillon cube in the water. Add the liquid to the pan.

Continue to cook over medium heat for 10 minutes, or until the liquid has evaporated. Stir frequently, especially during the last few minutes.

Polka Time at the Old Dance Hall

Whenever we go to San Antonio, Texas, we visit the River Walk. The meandering path along the water with outdoor cafes is a great place to relax and watch the tour boats go by.

One time, we took a side trip to Gruene, a town just north of San Antonio. The oldest, continually operating dance hall in the state of Texas was built in Gruene in the 1880s. It and the adjoining saloon provided entertainment for the local farming community. Cold beer and live music are still available almost every night of the week.

The well-worn, well-stomped dance floor was a launching pad for the careers of Lyle Lovett, George Strait, and Hal Ketchum. Bo Diddley, The Dixie Chicks, Jerry Lee Lewis, Garth Brooks, and Willie Nelson have all left their mark on the small, crude stage at the back of the hall.

Gruene's number one cash crop was cotton. The town flourished until the boll weevil and the Depression caused economic disaster. Apart from the dance hall, Greune became a ghost town until 1975 when buildings were restored. Today, the stools at the soda fountain in the first mercantile store are a perfect spot to sit, sip, and step into the past.

The first settlers in the area were German farmers. The sweet-sour flavor and the aroma of this potato salad are fine examples of German culinary creativity. Dished up with sausage, sauerkraut, and beer, this hot German potato salad would have been a welcome treat after a Saturday night polka dance at the old Greune hall.

Hot German Potato Salad

(Serves 4)

¼ pound	113 g	bacon, diced
5	5	potatoes, washed and peeled
¼	¼	apple, finely diced
¼ cup	60 ml	finely diced celery
2 tablespoons	30 ml	chopped Spanish onion
¼ cup	60 ml	green relish
½ cup	120 ml	apple juice or apple cider
¼ cup	60 ml	apple cider vinegar
⅛ teaspoon	0.63 ml	black pepper
¼ teaspoon	1.25 ml	salt
1 teaspoon	5 ml	white sugar
2 tablespoons	30 ml	chopped fresh parsley

Fry the diced bacon until it is crisp. Transfer the cooked bacon to a paper towel to absorb the grease.

Boil the peeled potatoes either whole or halved, until they are cooked. Be careful not to overcook them or they will fall apart when sliced.

Drain the potatoes in a colander. When they are cool enough to touch, cut them into ½-inch cubes. Set the potato cubes aside in a covered bowl.

In a saucepan, combine the bacon, apple, celery, onion, relish, apple juice, cider vinegar, pepper, salt, and sugar. Bring the mixture to a boil. Stir over medium-high heat for about 10 minutes.

Pour the hot mixture over the cubed potatoes. Stir gently.

Serve the potato salad hot with parsley sprinkled on top.

The Trading Tradition of Teslin, Yukon

In Teslin, Yukon, population 450, the Alaska Highway meanders between the past and the present.

The First Nations village is tucked away from the highway along the waters of Nisutlin Bay and Teslin Lake. It was here that Tlingit traders from the Alaskan coast swapped fish oil and seaweed with the Tutchone and Tagish people of the Yukon interior. In return they received meat, clothing, and furs. The log trading post built in 1903 still serves the community. It is well stocked with fishing and hunting gear, groceries and clothing, spices, and small hardware.

The modern Yukon Motel and RV Park is across the Alaska Highway from the village. Flower boxes hang from windowsills. RVs overlook Teslin Lake from grassy sites. A restaurant and gas pumps serve locals and travelers. The washrooms are spotless and it would be difficult to find a cigarette butt in the gravel parking lot.

The Yukon Wildlife Gallery adjoins the motel and restaurant. It offers a rare look at many of the wildlife species of the Yukon. We gasped at the realism of the stuffed animals and birds. Grizzlies, caribou, wolves, foxes, owls, moose, and musk ox look alive and eager to be out in the wide-open spaces.

We created this bok choy recipe to make a dish that is worth enjoying and then trading, in the style of the original nomadic First Nations people of Teslin.

Braised Bok Choy

(Serves 3 or 4)

4 cups	960 ml	chopped bok choy
2 tablespoons	30 ml	sesame oil
4 tablespoons	60 ml	tarragon vinegar
1	1	vegetable bouillon cube

Wash the bok choy and trim away the large leafy parts keeping the white and a little green. Chop the bok choy into bite-sized pieces.

Place the oil in a deep frying pan. Heat the oil to medium-high and add the bok choy. Stir and toss until a few of the pieces are browned and all of them are slightly tender.

Add the tarragon vinegar and the bouillon cube and stir well to dissolve the bouillon cube and blend the flavors. Cook on low heat for 3 minutes and serve. This dish can be prepared ahead and reheated.

The World's Smallest Desert

The 642-acre (260-hectare) Carcross Desert is affectionately known as the smallest desert in the world. It's located on the Klondike Highway in Canada's Yukon, less than an hour's drive from Whitehorse en route to Skagway, Alaska.

Thousands of people stop at the Carcross Desert every year. They roll down a car window, take a photo, and drive on. They fail to experience a unique northern phenomenon because they don't get out of their vehicles. We hiked across the desert sand and climbed to the top of the dunes to find a spectacular view of Lake Bennett, the waterway that played an important role in the historical Klondike Gold Rush.

The Carcross Desert's dunes rise in an area that was originally covered by a large glacial lake. As the glaciers retreated, causing lower water levels, sandy lake-bottom material was left behind. Strong prevailing winds have constantly worked the sand, making it difficult for vegetation to become established.

Many people don't like brussels sprouts, the small cabbage and member of the mustard family that is a good source of vitamins A and C. Like those who don't make an effort to enjoy the world's smallest desert, they miss the opportunity to experience something spectacular.

Brussels Sprouts with Appeal

(Serves 2 or 3)

8 to 10	8 to 10	brussels sprouts
½	½	slice cooked bacon
2 tablespoons	30 ml	finely diced onion
2 tablespoons	30 ml	mayonnaise
2 tablespoons	30 ml	sweet pickle juice
½ teaspoon	2.5 ml	dry mustard

Wash and trim the brussels sprouts. Place them in a saucepan and cover them with water. Cook over medium-high heat until almost tender.

Chop the cooked bacon. Heat a small frying pan. Add the bacon and onion to the pan. Cook over medium heat until the onion is translucent. Turn off the heat.

Combine the mayonnaise, pickle juice, and dry mustard in a small bowl and mix thoroughly.

Drain the brussels sprouts and place them in a serving dish.

Return the bacon-and-onion mixture to medium heat. Add the mayonnaise mixture. Heat until warm.

Pour the mixture over the hot brussels sprouts and serve.

Wild Burros Would Like This Dish

Oatman, Arizona, is a ghost town located on historic U.S. Route 66. It is the last stop in Arizona before entering the Mojave Desert of California. The town was founded around 1906. In the 1930s it produced over 36 million dollars in gold. In 1942, the U.S. Congress declared that gold mining was no longer essential to the war effort and the last remaining mines were closed.

The interesting thing about Oatman is that when the prospectors and miners vacated the town, they released their burros. The descendants of those animals roam wild in the surrounding hills. Some of these burros have moved back into town. We met Strawberry, Sarah Bell, Springtime, Aqua, Stormy, Willow, Sassy, Jesse and Buck on the main street. The tourists feed them popcorn and carrots.

We created the following vegetable dish for people. The burros of Oatman would like it, too.

Orange Mixed Vegetables

(Serves 4)

1	1	sweet potato
1	1	zucchini
2	2	carrots
35	35	fresh green beans
¾ cup	180 ml	water
2 tablespoons	30 ml	soy sauce
1 tablespoon	15 ml	brown sugar
1 tablespoon	15 ml	cornstarch
¼ teaspoon	1.25 ml	salt
2 tablespoons	30 ml	water
¼ cup	60 ml	lightly salted peanuts
¾ cup	180 ml	canned mandarin orange slices, drained

Peel and cut the sweet potato into ¹/₂-inch cubes. Cut the zucchini into ¹/₄-inch rounds. Cut the carrot into ¹/₄-inch coins. Trim the ends of the green beans and cut the beans into 1-inch pieces.

Bring the water and sweet potato to a boil in a saucepan. Turn the heat down and simmer for 5 minutes.

Add the zucchini, carrot, and green beans. Cover and simmer for 5 minutes, or until the vegetables are crispy-tender.

In a small bowl, mix the soy sauce, brown sugar, cornstarch, salt, and water. Stir until smooth. Add to the vegetables.

Cook and stir until the liquid thickens.

Add the peanuts and the drained mandarin orange slices. Stir once or twice to heat the peanuts and orange slices. Serve.

Nature's Show of Autumn Colors

The Algoma Central Railway not only provides a service to visitors who want to witness the spectacular fall colors of the Agawa Canyon, it is the only means of access to some of the remote communities of Ontario's north.

We pulled out of the station in Sault Ste. Marie, Ontario, aboard the Algoma Central Railway in the early morning mist, with twenty-three railway cars carrying fourteen hundred people. We crept through tunnels of evergreens, glided over towering trestles, and slithered past serene lakes and around granite rock formations. All around us, orange, red, and yellow leaves decorated the countryside.

At mile 31.5 out of Sault Ste. Marie, the thick bush opened to the mountain village of Searchmont. As the train slowly approached the settlement, we passed a small, one-room schoolhouse. Outside, in the morning mist, the students of Searchmont School stood waving at the passengers on the train. They held large cardboard signs that spelled out the words, "good morning." Up to one hundred thousand visitors, from all over the world, travel past the schoolhouse every year.

At noon, 114 miles (183 kilometers) north of Sault Ste. Marie, we disembarked to find picnic tables along the banks of the Agawa River. There were waterfalls to discover, hiking trails to climb, and maple trees to photograph.

A man who had stepped off the train ahead of us, looked around at the spectacular view, turned to his wife, and said, "Is this it?" If only he had said something earlier, we could have left him at the casino or the mall in Sault Ste. Marie.

Autumn colors may not be everyone's idea of beauty, but we can't imagine a more artistic show than the one that nature provides for us every year.

Orange, Red, Yellow, and Green Stir Fry

(Serves 5 or 6)

3 tablespoons	45 ml	balsamic vinegar
3 tablespoons	45 ml	orange juice
¼ cup	60 ml	olive oil
1 tablespoon	15 ml	finely chopped grated orange zest
90	90	small sugar snap peas
1	1	small red pepper, cut into thin strips
1	1	small yellow pepper, cut into thin strips
		salt
		pepper
1	1	navel orange

Combine balsamic vinegar, orange juice, olive oil, and grated orange peel in a container. Cover and refrigerate for 2 hours to blend the flavors.

Transfer the orange juice mixture to a large frying pan over high heat. When the liquid is bubbling, add the snap peas and the red and yellow pepper strips.

Stir the vegetables over high heat for 2 to 3 minutes to coat them with the marinade. Sprinkle them lightly with salt and pepper.

Transfer the vegetables and the liquid from the pan to a serving bowl.

Cut the orange into 6 wedges to garnish the outside edges of the bowl and serve.

A Recipe for Success

We owned and operated restaurants for almost twenty years. We can testify to the fact that, once in the food business, a person is in it forever, physically or mentally. Sometimes, in our travels, we see a building or a setting that we think would be perfect for a restaurant. Then, we remind each other of the hours and hours of work involved in running one.

When we sold our first restaurant, after five years of not knowing what day of the week it was, we promised ourselves that we would never run a restaurant again. Within a year, we were back in the business. One time, the building enticed us; another time, it was the location. Once, it was an opportunity to purchase an existing business that we just couldn't resist. Another time, it was the opportunity to use our imaginations to build and equip a business starting with nothing but bare walls and a floor. We sold one restaurant only to start another. Now, we are often busy as restaurant consultants. Our years of hands-on experience have given us a recipe for success that we share with disgruntled restaurateurs.

We have a cheesecake recipe that brings back sweet memories of our first restaurant. During a trip to Europe, before we locked ourselves into the food service business, we met Annie Grant from Australia. Annie later came to work for us, and her cheesecake recipe became a hit with our regular customers.

Annie's Pineapple Cheesecake

(Serves 12)

9 ounces	250 g	coconut cookies
½ cup	120 ml	melted butter or margarine
1½ teaspoons	7.5 ml	ground cinnamon
19 ounces	570 ml	canned crushed pineapple
9 ounces	255 g	cream cheese
10 ounces	300 ml	sweetened condensed milk
3 tablespoons	45 ml	lemon juice from concentrate
		whipped cream

Crush the cookies to a fine texture using a food processor or rolling pin.

Put the butter in a small saucepan and melt it over low heat.

Combine the cookie crumbs and the melted butter in a bowl, mix thoroughly, and place in a large glass or ceramic pie plate. Spread the crumbs to create a pie shell, pressing them firmly to the bottom and sides until smooth and even.

Sprinkle the cinnamon evenly over the bottom of the newly created shell. Place the shell in the freezer for at least 30 minutes to set.

Place the pineapple in a sieve for at least 20 minutes to drain. Discard the juice.

Remove the cream cheese from the refrigerator to soften. (Do not use cream cheese spread.) When the cream cheese is soft, add it to the condensed milk in a mixing bowl and beat until smooth.

Add the drained pineapple and lemon juice and beat for 3 or 4 minutes. Do not skimp on the lemon juice because it enhances the flavor and helps set the cheesecake.

Pour the mixture into the chilled crust. Refrigerate the cheesecake for at least 1 hour before serving (or freeze for future indulgence).

Serve with whipped cream.

This Dessert Was Made for Our Spanish Teachers

In 1959, Olinette ("Ollie") Everard left the comfort of her home in the United States to travel to the southern cities and isolated jungle villages of Mexico and Latin America. She learned Spanish so she could teach the local people how to read and write in their own language. She had no one working with her, no organization behind her, and no pledged support. For twenty-one years, Ollie relied on contributions from friends and acquaintances to support her in her mission to help the underprivileged.

Ollie met Betty Stoudt in Guadalajara in 1969. Betty was studying Spanish, and Ollie was teaching a literacy workshop. Betty joined Ollie in her mission to eradicate illiteracy. Betty had previously worked for Wycliffe Bible Translators, an organization that helped to create a written language and basic grammar for the San Miguel el Grande Mixtec Indians. Betty, an American, had learned to speak Mixtec. She distributed bibles to the Indians in Oaxaca, Mexico.

In 1981, Betty and Ollie returned to the United States. In their retirement years, they teach Winter Texans in the Rio Grande Valley to speak and read Spanish. They were our Spanish teachers, and they were very patient.

They gave us several sweet Texas grapefruits from the tree in their yard. We used those grapefruit to create this recipe.

Delicioso Fresh Grapefruit Delight

(Serves 6 to 8)

36	36	*large marshmallows*
5	5	*sweet red grapefruits*
½ cup	120 ml	*sweet red grapefruit juice*
1 cup	240 ml	*whipping cream*

Cut the marshmallows in half and set aside.

Peel the grapefruit and separate the fillets by first cutting away both ends of the grapefruit with a sharp knife. Place the fruit flat end down on a counter and cut away the peel from top to bottom along the curvature of the fruit, removing all the white. Cut along both membranes of a section of the grapefruit, and then turn the knife to loosen the fillet and lift it out. Remove all the fillets the same way. Cut each fillet in half, crosswise, if they are larger than bite-sized. You should have about 2½ cups.

Place the sections in a sieve to drain excess liquid. Do not squeeze the grapefruit sections. Reserve the juice.

Measure the reserved juice and top it off with grapefruit juice in order to make ½ cup.

Place the marshmallows and half of the grapefruit juice in a saucepan and stir constantly over medium heat until the marshmallows are completely melted. Set aside and let cool to room temperature.

Combine the remaining half of the grapefruit juice and the grapefruit sections.

Whip the cream until it's thick and holding its shape.

Fold the whipped cream, grapefruit sections, and melted marshmallows together in a large bowl. Pour into serving dishes and refrigerate overnight to set.

Dive into This Tasty Orange Pie

Greek spongers came to Tarpon Springs, Florida, in 1905 and developed the world's largest sponge industry.

On a boat tour of the local sponge beds, we watched a sponger jump overboard wearing over one hundred pounds of diving suit, helmet, neck weights, and lead boots. He surfaced in his orange suit with a perfect sponge, which he had snatched from its bed beneath the water's surface.

The following orange pie is sweet, easy, and delicious. Dive in.

Orange Cream Pie

(Serves 8)

3 tablespoons	45 ml	cream cheese
1	1	Graham cracker pie crust
3 cups	720 ml	mandarin oranges
1 cup	240 ml	orange juice
3 ounces	85 g	orange Jell-O
		whipped cream

Spread the cream cheese over the bottom of the pie crust and set it in the freezer to chill.

Place the mandarin orange sections in a sieve to drain. Discard the syrup. Gently press the orange sections to remove any excess juice.

Heat the orange juice in a saucepan just to the point of boiling.

Add the Jell-O to the orange juice and stir until the Jell-O is completely dissolved.

Place the Jell-O mixture in the freezer to cool.

Add the orange sections to the cooled Jell-O. Mix well and chill until almost completely set.

Stir the mixture again and place it in the pie crust.

Cover the entire surface of the pie with whipped cream and refrigerate over night to set.

Spring Break Is Party Time on South Padre Island

Spring Break on South Padre Island, Texas, increases the normal population of two thousand people into a crowd of mostly under-twenty-five-year-olds. According to a local, spring break is bikini break. Traffic is so heavy that beach parties and T-shirt contests are best witnessed from a boat, especially by those who are too old to be in the middle of the action. Businesses that offer outdoor activities like windsurfing, snorkeling, dune buggy riding, horseback riding, and floating tricycles are booked to capacity. T-shirt shops, seashell stores, and bars are jammed.

The South Padre Island Convention and Visitors Bureau sponsors a *Guide for Island Life During Spring Break*. Basic tips are given to visiting students on how to avoid sunburn, rip tides, disturbing the locals, and arrest.

Spring time is party time on South Padre Island, but anytime is trifle time. The following recipe can be easily scaled down or increased to accommodate any size group. Make it ahead of time, and enjoy the party.

Orange Trifle

(Serves 4 or 5)

4 ½ teaspoons	22.5 ml	custard powder
1 ¼ cups	300 ml	milk
4 ½ teaspoons	22.5 ml	sugar
1	1	small package orange Jell-O
1 cup	240 ml	whipping cream
½ teaspoon	2.5 ml	sugar
10 ounces	300 ml	mandarin orange sections
1	1	small pound cake or sponge cake
		rum flavoring
½	½	square semisweet chocolate

Dissolve the custard powder in a little of the cold milk. Stir until it is smooth.

Heat the remaining milk to boiling. As it heats, stir in the sugar.

Add the dissolved custard powder to the hot milk, stirring constantly. Boil the mixture for 1 minute. Pour it into a bowl and set it in the refrigerator to cool.

Make the orange Jell-O according to package's instructions and place it in the refrigerator to set.

Whip the cream. Just before it stiffens, whip in the sugar. Set the whipped cream in the refrigerator.

Drain the mandarin oranges. Reserve 3 sections for garnish.

Slice the cake and place half of it in the bottom of a large, clear bowl.

Sprinkle the cake with the rum flavoring, being careful not to oversaturate.

Spoon half of the Jell-O over the cake. Be sure that some of the Jell-O is visible at the sides of the bowl.

Pour half of the custard over the Jell-O and spread it to the edges, letting it seep down into the cake.

Cover the custard with half the whipped cream.

Scatter half the mandarin oranges on top of the whipped cream.

Repeat the process with the other half of the cake, the Jell-O, custard, and mandarin oranges. Cover the mandarin oranges with the remaining whipped cream.

Arrange the 3 reserved orange sections in a design on top of the whipped cream layer.

Sprinkle grated or crumbled chocolate over the whipped cream. Place the trifle in the refrigerator to chill.

Walking a Mile in Elvis's Shoes

Elvis Presley died August 16, 1977. In 1995, we visited Graceland, Elvis's mansion in Memphis, Tennessee. Until then, our impression of Graceland was black velvet paintings, pink Cadillacs, gaudy wrought-iron gates, and women swarming the grounds. We were wrong.

Graceland was Elvis's home. It stands at the top of a hill, tall and white. Its pillars and windows look down the curved driveway across the lawns through the oak trees to the street. We barely noticed the wrought-iron gates.

Inside Graceland we felt as though we had entered Elvis's personal life. In the dining room as we stood at the rope barrier behind Elvis's chair, we saw the room from his perspective. It was warm, bright, and open. We would have felt comfortable sitting at his table.

The Lisa Marie was something else again. The plane that Elvis named after his daughter displayed the luxury of its time. Sky phones, three televisions, a quadraphonic stereo system, and gold-plated seat belt buckles were part of the package. There was even a queen bed with a seat belt and a galley with a stove, a refrigerator, and a built-in coffee maker. Restrooms had brass fixtures imported from Spain and twenty-four-karat gold flecks in the sinks. The airplane required a crew of four. In an onboard video, one of the pilots told the story of Elvis taking a group of his friends on a late-night flight to Colorado. Elvis knew a place in Denver that had the best peanut butter sandwiches.

Like the following recipe, some things are worth going the extra mile.

Peach Dream

(Serves 6)

½ cup	120 ml	soft cream cheese
1 tablespoon	15 ml	light mayonnaise
1½ teaspoons	7.5 ml	vanilla
¼ teaspoon	1.25 ml	salt
¼ teaspoon	1.25 ml	white pepper
1 cup	240 ml	almond slivers, lightly toasted
6	6	canned clingstone peach halves

Mash the cream cheese and mayonnaise together with a fork. Add the vanilla, salt, and pepper. Stir until the combination is smooth. Set aside.

Place the almond slivers in a dry frying pan over low heat. Constantly stir until they are very lightly toasted. Let cool. As they cool, remove any slivers that are too dark, because they will taste bitter. Set 6 almond slivers aside for garnish.

When cool, stir the toasted almonds into the cream cheese mixture.

Spoon the nutty-creamy filling into the center of each peach. Refrigerate.

Garnish each serving with a toasted almond sliver.

Four and Twenty Grackles Baked in a Pie

The grackle is a member of the American blackbird family. There is no such thing as one grackle sitting in a tree by itself in the Rio Grande Valley of Texas. There are always hundreds and even thousands of grackles at a time. These birds of a feather stick together. Sleek creatures, with iridescent, black plumage, long tails, and wild eyes, they tend to gather on overhead wires and palm trees around sunset. They don't chirp or sing. Their sound is much like a squeaky, rusty door hinge.

At one RV park in Texas, the manager had a system to keep the birds from settling in the magnificent palm trees that line the property. Just at sunset, an oversized speaker broadcasted the sound of a grackle being chased, caught, and eaten by a hawk. The sound was amusing to humans but the grackles fled down the road to the trees at the local K-Mart store.

We've heard that the grackle population is spreading northward. A recipe for four and twenty blackbirds baked in a pie might be appropriate, but the thought of grackle pie doesn't appeal to us.

Lemon Marshmallow Pie

(Serves 8)

8 ounces	227 g	frozen whipped topping
1	1	Graham cracker pie crust
10	10	lemons
8 ounces	227 g	miniature marshmallows
3 ounces	85 g	lemon Jell-O
1 cup	240 ml	whipping cream

Remove the frozen whipped topping from the freezer to soften.

Peel the lemons removing as much of the white portion of the peel as possible. Cut along each membrane and remove the lemon segments.

Place the segments in a sieve to drain. Remove any seeds and remaining membrane. Reserve ¼ cup lemon juice.

Chop the fruit into small pieces and return the pieces to the sieve. Press the lemon pieces to force any remaining juice out of the lemon flesh.

Place the marshmallows in a saucepan over low heat. Add the lemon juice and stir constantly to prevent sticking. When the marshmallows are melted, remove the saucepan from the heat and add the Jell-O powder. Stir until it is completely dissolved. Place the Jell-O mixture in a bowl.

Set the Jell-O in the refrigerator until the mixture is almost firm.

Fold the softened whipped topping and the chopped, drained lemon flesh into the Jell-O mixture. Stir until the ingredients are well mixed then pour the mixture into the pie crust.

Place the pie in the refrigerator to set. Whip cream.

When the pie is set, cover the top with whipped cream.

Any leftover pie filling can be spooned into individual dessert dishes.

Wal-Mart Arrives in Whitehorse

One of the biggest events in Whitehorse, Yukon, in 2002 was the arrival of a Wal-Mart store. People from the far north chartered airplanes in order to witness the grand opening. Yukoners from outlying districts made a special trip to town. Local students received a day out of school to work on Wal-Mart assignments. All the hotels in town were fully booked.

The Wal-Mart store not only introduced the box store phenomenon to Whitehorse, it also brought a new lifestyle into the heart of the town. Up until the opening of Wal-Mart, RVers parked their motorhomes, fifth wheels, and trailers in private campgrounds and territorial parks. Suddenly, on any given day, forty to sixty recreational vehicles were parking overnight in the oversized Wal-Mart parking lot.

For years, throughout the United States, Wal-Mart has had an unofficial corporate policy of allowing boondocking on their property. No electricity, no water, and no sewer facilities. Most RVers spend a night in a Wal-Mart parking lot when it is either too late or too dark to locate a campground. They do their shopping at the Wal-Mart store and often spend more than they would have spent in an RV park. However, there are people who push policies to the limits and make Wal-Mart their destination. They put their jacks down, their television antennas up, their awnings and lawn chairs out. They set up their barbecues and hang their laundry out to dry. Camp Wal-Mart.

This dessert is ideal accompanied by a cup of coffee under the awning of an RV.

Cherry Basmati Rice Pudding

(Serves 6)

4 cups	960 ml	skim milk
½ cup	120 ml	long-grain basmati rice
1	1	pinch salt
2	2	egg yolks
2 teaspoons	10 ml	vanilla
5 tablespoons	75 ml	sugar
3¾ cups	900 ml	canned pitted Bing cherries
		whipped cream (optional)

Pour the milk into a saucepan. Add the rice and salt. Stir. Bring to a boil, then cover and cook at a slow boil for 15 minutes.

Remove the lid and simmer for 10 minutes more, stirring frequently, until the rice is tender and the mixture has thickened.

Beat the egg yolks with a fork. Add the vanilla and sugar to the eggs.

Drain the cherries. Reserve 6 for garnish. Cut each of the remaining cherries in half. Place the cut cherries on a paper towel to remove any excess moisture. Stir the cut cherries into the egg mixture.

Add the egg-cherry mixture to the hot rice over medium-low heat. Mix well, stirring constantly, for 2 minutes, until thickened.

Spoon the rice pudding into serving dishes and serve either warm or cold. If serving cold, cover and refrigerate until ready to serve.

Garnish with a cherry.

Red, Redder, and Reddest

The grapefruit has an obscure origin but was thought to be discovered in Barbados during the 1750s. Years later, research confirmed that the grapefruit was a hybrid of the sweet orange and the pummelo, a pear-shaped citrus fruit with a thick rind. A Jamaican farmer created the name "grapefruit" because of its grape-like cluster on the trees.

It is believed that the grapefruit was introduced to the United States in the 1800s, in the form of seeds transported by either Spanish or French settlers to Florida. Eventually, grapefruit made its way to south Texas, most likely by visiting Spanish missionaries.

Initial grapefruit plantings in Texas were the white varieties, followed by pinks. Around the time of the great stock market crash in 1929, the discovery of red grapefruit growing on a pink grapefruit tree gave rise to the Texas Red Grapefruit Industry. In time, redder mutations were found in numerous groves.

Following the heavy freezes in 1949, 1951, and 1962, Texas eliminated its white and pink varieties and set out to establish a reputation for growing red grapefruit. Again, mutations appeared on the trees, each one a deeper shade of red than the one before. A decision was made to differentiate the Texas sweet red grapefruit from the others on the market by registering them under three trademark categories, Flame, Ruby-Sweet, and Rio Star, otherwise known as red, redder, and reddest.

It was in south Texas that we first heard about grapefruit pie.

Grapefruit Pie

(Serves 8)

8	8	sweet red grapefruit
1 cup	240 ml	white sugar
1¾ cups	420 ml	water
2 tablespoons	30 ml	cornstarch
¼ teaspoon	1.25 ml	salt
3 ounces	85 g	strawberry Jell-O
1	1	baked pie crust
		whipped cream

Peel the grapefruit and separate the fillets by first removing both ends of a grapefruit with a sharp knife. Place the fruit on a cutting board with the flat, cut end down. Cut away the peel from top to bottom along the curvature of the fruit, removing all the white pulp. Cut along both membranes of a section of the grapefruit, then, turn the knife to loosen the fillet and lift it out. Remove all the fillets the same way. You should have about 4¹/₂ cups.

Place the grapefruit fillets in a sieve to drain. They must be drained well. The longer they sit in the sieve the better. Place a bowl under the sieve to catch the fresh juice. Although the juice is not used in this recipe, it is good to drink.

Combine the sugar, water, cornstarch, and salt in a saucepan and stir or whisk until the cornstarch is dissolved.

Cook and stir until the mixture is clear and just reaches a boil. Do not allow it to bubble.

Remove the saucepan from the heat and add the Jell-O powder. Stir until the Jell-O is dissolved.

Chill until the mixture is almost set. It should reach the texture of jelly.

Fold the grapefruit fillets into the Jell-O mixture. Pour the mixture into the baked pie crust.

Cover the entire surface of the pie with whipped topping to seal the pie.

Refrigerate overnight to set.

There Are Strange Things Done in the Midnight Sun

If the well-known Yukon poet Robert Service were alive today he might see an even stranger sight than the cremation of Sam McGee: the Sourtoe Cocktail.

What we saw in the Downtown Hotel in Dawson City was the queerest thing we ever did see. We watched people drop a pickled toe into their drink, raise their glass, and knock it back as the toe slid to their lips. To join the exclusive Sourtoe Cocktail Club, the drinker's lips must touch the toe.

The Sourtoe has been a Dawson City, Yukon, tradition since 1973. We were told that it was created when a miner's toe was found preserved in a jar of alcohol. Since that day almost fifteen thousand people from around the world have taken the challenge of drinking down their brandy or beer along with the petrified appendage. They have a certificate to show for it, and their names are listed in the official Sourtoe logbook. The first toe used for the cocktail lasted roughly fifteen years, until someone either stole it or swallowed it. Since then, some members of the Sourtoe Cocktail Club have willed their toes to the hotel. A health inspector concluded that because the toe was pickled there was nothing wrong with it. He said it wasn't the toe that would make people sick, it was the quantity of alcohol they drank along with it.

We declined the Sourtoe, however, we would never say no to this hot cranberry orange grog.

Hot Cranberry-Orange Grog

(Serves 4)

¼ cup	60 ml	currants
¼ teaspoon	1.25 ml	cardamom
2 tablespoons	30 ml	fresh lemon juice
1 cup	240 ml	orange juice
4 cups	960 ml	cranberry cocktail
½	½	cinnamon stick
1	1	slice orange
pinch	pinch	ground cloves

Bring the currants, cardamom, lemon juice, orange juice, cranberry cocktail, and cinnamon stick to a slow simmer in a saucepan over low heat. Stir once or twice.

Cut the orange slice in half. Rub the ground cloves on one half of the orange slice and add it to the simmering pot. Simmer for 30 minutes.

Discard the cinnamon stick and the orange slice.

Ladle the grog into mugs. Cut 4 triangles from the remaining half slice orange and place 1 in each mug as garnish.

It is not necessary to increase the spices if the liquid in this recipe is doubled. Leave it to steep on the heat about 10 minutes longer to get the full flavor of the spices. The grog can be made in advance, refrigerated, and then reheated just prior to serving.

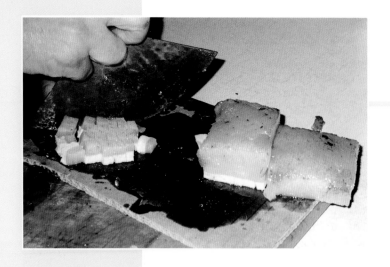

It's a Different Kind of Diet in the North

It was mid-August when we took a thirty-minute flight from Inuvik to Tuktoyaktuk, Northwest Territories. If it had been later in the year, when the temperature drops way below freezing, we could have driven the ice road. Our flight was shared with two other passengers and a large pile of mailbags destined for the remote village on the shore of the Beaufort Sea.

After we had dipped our toes in the Arctic Ocean, Maureen Pokiak invited us into her home to sample authentic Inuit dishes. For starters, we tasted migu, the air-cured red meat from the backbone of the beluga whale, muktuk, the boiled layer of the whale between the outer skin and the inner blubber, and bipsi, air-dried white fish. The main dish was caribou soup and bannock.

Maureen was originally from Saskatchewan. She went to Tuktoyaktuk in 1974 as a schoolteacher, married James, and adopted his way of life. Maureen and James harvest 70 percent of their food off the land. In one year, their family of five lives on 20 to 25 caribou, 1 or 2 beluga whales, 60 to 80 geese, as well as fish and berries. In late August, the Pokiaks load their sled dogs and their supplies onto a bush plane and leave the village of Tuktoyaktuk for their camp out on the frozen tundra. Their supplies are limited to fish nets, guns, ammunition, traps, and a very basic food supply consisting of salt, flour, and whale oil. For their meals, they fish, pick berries and hunt caribou. In September, between 2,000 and 3,000 caribou walk through their camp. Maureen said that in the silence of the Arctic, they hear the caribou coming. They only kill what they will eat.

This hot apple cider is a good warm-up drink, especially for anyone out on the frozen tundra.

Hot Spiced Apple Cider

(Serves 4)

6 cups	1.4 L	sweet apple cider
1	1	cinnamon stick, broken into pieces, plus more for garnish
1 teaspoon	5 ml	whole cloves
¼ teaspoon	1.25 ml	ground nutmeg
1 tablespoon	15 ml	honey

In a saucepan, combine the cider, cinnamon, cloves, nutmeg, and honey.

Bring the ingredients to a slow simmer over low heat and simmer for 30 minutes.

Remove the cinnamon stick pieces and the whole cloves.

Ladle the hot apple cider into mugs and serve with a cinnamon stick garnish.

Palm Trees in the Middle of the Desert

Green trees are a rare sight in the Arizona desert in January. When we heard that the only native palm trees in Arizona were hidden high in the rugged canyons of the Kofa National Wildlife Refuge, between Yuma and Quartzsite, we joined friends for an adventure. About forty-two California fan palms nest in a narrow crevice in the volcanic rock in Palm Canyon.

Reaching those majestic, green palms was exciting. We stretched between footholds. We squeezed between rock faces. Our reward was lunch under the palms.

We also experienced jeeping in Arizona. A ride in a four-wheel-drive vehicle took us over rocks, up hills, and along dry riverbeds to impossible places for an ordinary car. Sitting in the back seat of the Jeep was like riding a bucking bronco.

No matter what the adventure in Arizona, we always carried water bottles. The air was consistently dry. The average yearly rainfall in Quartzsite is only 4.37 inches (11 centimeters). Just the thought of the desert is enough to make a person thirsty for a cool tomato vegetable juice.

Tomato Vegetable Juice

(Serves 3)

4 cups	960 ml	canned diced tomatoes with liquid
1	1	Spanish onion, peeled and finely diced
2	2	sweet red peppers, seeds removed, finely diced
½	½	stalk celery, finely diced
4 teaspoons	20 ml	sugar

In a large saucepan, combine the diced tomatoes with liquid, diced onion, diced red peppers, and diced celery. Slowly boil the vegetables for 15 minutes.

Remove from the heat and strain to remove the pulp.

Return the strained liquid to a saucepan and add the sugar.

Boil for 5 minutes.

Pour the juice into a pitcher and refrigerate.

Acknowledgments

If there are any mistakes in this cookbook, it is not our fault. Blame our proofreaders, Vicky Lawrence, Judy Johnston, Bob Johnston, and Joan Smith. They will tell you that this book was edited under duress. This is correct. In less than a week, our dear friends checked each of our stories and recipes for interest, flow, humor, clarity, grammar, and spelling. They also checked each recipe for the metric equivalents.

When the manuscript came back from our proofreaders, we discovered that Joan loves commas and that Bob, Judy, and Vicky go "commatose" at the sight of them. From reports, it appears that we drove at least one of our proofreaders to drink.

We received the following email from Judy who shared the editing job with her sister, Vicky, and husband, Bob. We had given them a deadline of Sunday night to proofread the cookbook. This message came to us on Saturday morning.

"Okay, you people are so asking for it. First of all, to call this a proofreading job was a misnomer. It is an editing and proofreading job and way bigger than we ever imagined. First we proofed copy. We only challenged each other a wee titch about grammar and appropriate uses of creative writing versus technical writing. Then we proofed the math. We debated about appropriate use of decimals. Then, when we discovered the context of measurements was sometimes questionable, we reproofed them with a fine-toothed comb. We argued until we found answers that seemed right to all of us. We edited and proofed and fought like cats and dogs most every hour that we weren't working, eating, or sleeping. Our goal was to finish it up by early Saturday morning so we could get on with other plans we had for the weekend.

"As I sat enjoying my second coffee Saturday morning, quietly and calmly finalizing the context of the measurements, I had that quiet confidence of someone who has worked hard, met her goals, and has her life under control. That's when Bob went online to pick up any emails that came in over the last twenty-four hours. He screamed in horror to Vicky and me when he saw that there was more editing to do. Well, to make a long story short, we screamed and ranted and then it turned violent. Vicky stormed out of the apartment, Bob washed his hands of the whole thing, and I am now drinking Baileys in my coffee, staring blankly and rocking myself back and forth, back and forth, back and forth...."

Joan, on the other hand, worked independently. Without influences, she came up with the following report. "I have been enjoying reading all of your stories, and the recipes really are wonderful. I hadn't really realized how many places you've been, and the interesting things you've done and fascinating people you've met. What a wonderful life! And, you've made it all come so alive in your stories. The reader can live vicariously through your words."

We thank you all for your kind and honest comments. You did a wonderful job and we're glad you are still our friends.

Thank you Judy, Vicky, and Bob for lending us your one-of-a-kind plates so we could add a special touch to the photography of the finished recipes.

This traveling lifestyle means we are constantly meeting new friends and leaving other friends behind. Maybe it's because we are away from our family and our oldest and dearest friends that we appreciate how well people treat us when we pull into their neighborhood or RV park. By the time we leave, whether it is a few days or a month later, we feel as though we have known them for a long time. We want to thank those people for taking us into their hearts and sharing their time with us.

And finally, thank you to everyone at home and on the road who has inspired us to create wonderful recipes.

Measurement Conversions

LIQUID MEASURE

teaspoons to milliliters (ml) .... multiply by 5
tablespoons to milliliters .... multiply by 15
fluid ounces to milliliters .... multiply by 30
cups (8 ounce) to milliliters .... multiply by 240
cups (8 ounce) to liters (l) .... multiply by 0.24
pints to liters .... multiply by 0.47
quarts to liters .... multiply by 0.95

1 U.S. gallon .... equals 3.84 liters

1 teaspoon .... 5 ml
2 teaspoons .... 10 ml
3 teaspoons (1 tablespoon) .... 15 ml
$1/4$ teaspoon .... 1.25 ml
$1/2$ teaspoon .... 2.5 ml
1 tablespoon (3 teaspoons or $1/2$ fluid ounce) .... 15 ml
2 tablespoons ($1/8$ cup or 1 fluid ounce) .... 30 ml
$1/2$ tablespoon (1 $1/2$ teaspoons) .... 7.5 ml
1 fluid ounce .... 30 ml
1 cup (8 fluid ounces or 16 tablespoons) .... 240 ml
$1/8$ cup (1 fluid ounce or 2 tablespoons) .... 30 ml
$1/4$ cup (2 fluid ounces or 4 tablespoons) .... 60 ml
$1/2$ cup (4 fluid ounces or 8 tablespoons) .... 120 ml
$3/4$ cup (6 fluid ounces or 12 tablespoons) .... 180 ml
4 cups .... 960 ml
5 cups .... (1200 ml) 1.2 liters

WEIGHT MEASURE

ounces to grams (g) .... multiply by 28.35
pounds to kilograms (kg) .... multiply by 0.4536

$1/2$ ounce .... 14.175 g
1 ounce .... 28.35 g
3 ounces .... 85 g
$1/4$ pound (4 ounces) .... 113.4 g
$1/2$ pound (8 ounces) .... 226.8 g
$3/4$ pound (12 ounces) .... 340.2 g
1 pound (16 ounces) .... 453.6 g
1 $1/2$ pounds .... 680 g
2.21 pounds .... (1000 g) 1 kg

Index

ANECDOTES